Eph... Th... Glory of God in the Christian Calling

W. O. Carver

BROADMAN PRESS
Nashville, Tennessee

4213-13
ISBN: 0-8054-1313-8

Paperback edition 1979

Dewey Decimal Classification: 227.5
Subject Headings: BIBLE. N. T. EPHESIANS

Library of Congress Catalog Card Number: 78-74597
Printed in the United States of America

Contents

ACKNOWLEDGMENTS

Appreciative acknowledgment is made to publishers and authors for permission to use materials in this work as follows:

To Charles Scribner's Sons for quotations from Abbott, in *International Critical Commentary,* New York, 1897, Introduction, pp. xxiv-xxix; to Yale University Press for brief sentences from *The Christian View of the World,* Blewett, 1912, chapters 1, 2; to Hodder and Stoughton for use of some paragraphs from "The Expositor's Bible," new editions, *Ephesians,* by Findlay; also, for quotations from Salmond in *The Expositor's Greek Testament;* further, for some use of Moffatt's new translation of the New Testament, specifically the use of the phrase "colony of heaven" in Philippians 3:20; to the University of Chicago Press for use of *The Meaning of Ephesians,* by Goodspeed, 1933; to Macmillan and Company for two quotations from *The Christian Ecclesia,* by Hort, London, 1897; to Kelly for use of Lidgett's *God in Christ Jesus,* London, 1915; to The Pilgrim Press, Boston, for use of Weymouth's *Modern Speech New Testament.*

In all cases credit is given wherever the material appears.

PREFACE

It is with deep gratitude that I anticipate the publication of this study of the Book of Ephesians. Early in my Bible studies and teaching I became enthusiastic over this most remarkable document. Through more than half a century I have followed up this interest with growing conviction of its importance for the gospel and kingdom of our Lord and Saviour Jesus Christ.

My gratitude is first of all to "the God and Father of our Lord and Saviour Jesus Christ," by whose grace we live and work; and to the Holy Spirit who sustains and guides in our efforts to understand and to share in the purpose and the work of "our great God and Saviour."

I am grateful to the many students who have shared my studies in classrooms, and to the large number of people who have shared briefer studies in assemblies and conferences; for by their persistent and gracious encouragement through many years they have stimulated me in carrying forward to completion the manuscript which is now to be published. I am grateful to the Broadman Press for undertaking to bring this project through to publication. Dr. and Mrs. Clyde T. Francisco have been good enough to go carefully through the proof sheets, detecting errors and making suggestions toward improvements in the form of the work.

Readers will find some original suggestions and some new interpretations in these studies. Some will find an interpretation of the Church and the churches which may arouse question. If so, I can only hope that they will give faithful consideration to determine whether the author has followed the mind of Paul under the lead of the Holy Spirit. I have no pride in originality and no desire for novelty. I do seek independent receptivity and frankness in expression as I seek to be an interpreter of the word and work of God.

The book is in sections which have been arranged in a somewhat logical order. Readers may take these sections in whatever order seems best. Many will be primarily interested in the expository Paraphrase.

For the most part the effort has been to study this supreme Epistle as the timeless revelation of the grace of God unto salvation, yet never without consciousness of the application to the conditions and needs of our own time. In humble prayer that the Spirit of God will use this volume for the better understanding, in some measure, of the meaning of the Christian movement in history it is submitted to "all who love our Lord Jesus Christ in complete sincerity."

W. O. CARVER

PUBLISHER'S NOTE

This book was first published in 1949 under the title *The Glory of God in the Christian Calling*. Although it received favorable critical response, it did not win the readership that was expected and eventually went out of print. For several years we have received persistent requests that it be republished. To reduce the page count, some material has been deleted: a section entitled "The Church in the Ecumenical Movement," which is now quite out of date, and the King James Version of Ephesians, which faced the "Author's Translation," page by page, in the first edition. The rest of the book appears as it was first published except for new page numbering. We are pleased to make available again this important interpretation of Ephesians by such a notable scholar.

BROADMAN PRESS

The Supreme Christian Document

The greatest piece of writing in all history is this Ephesian Epistle. In it the constructive organization of human experience, human idealism, human hope reaches the highest point of response to the approach of God in revealing himself to the understanding and the life of man. Here "the divine-human encounter" that is the abiding history of the human race is outlined in amazing completeness. Here are both the essential and characteristic Christian experiences, and Christianity's principles in moral and ethical application.

All Scripture is superhuman in the important sense that it is the inspired formulation in human language of experiences and insights at the high level of communication of God to human personality and of human response at its best under the illumination and the lift of the grace of God. There must be varieties in quality and extent of such converse of God in the Spirit with man's spirit. Occasions, needs, purposes, and capacities will vary, and the ranges of revelation will be many.

God speaks in varying methods and measures through men whom he makes prophets—confidantes and spokesmen, mouthpieces of God—to make known his will and his way in the world of reality, the world of truth, the history of humanity. In every revelation the prophet is in some degree lifted out of the human and time context and is made to speak from without to men in that context. The prophet will usually see a relatively limited application of his message. For him to see too far might mean that he would overlook the specific purpose of his word from God. Always he is sure that it is a word from God, and he is convinced that it has eternal significance. Exactly what that wider significance may be he may not know. Always the prophet is aware of having been caught up in the stream of the divine purpose and power and of being "borne along by the Holy Spirit." Out of this conviction he speaks. The stretches of this stream of revelation and plan of which his word is a part, and the flood tides of its expansion may be wholly beyond the prophet's ken.

The purpose of God in the revealing message is in the widest sense always the same. The specific purposes of the individual revelations must be various, else they would not be effective. From time to time, as the unfolding work of God progresses, the depths and heights, the breadths and lengths of his age-long purposes may be—and have been—made known in amazing measure to chosen spokesmen in order that they might mark out the lines in which "through the ages one increasing purpose runs." These are "the friends" of God to whom his secrets are communicated in stewardship for mankind.

Moses was such a prophet. Through him God has marked the lines of the moral laws which lie at the center of social life and constitute the reinforcing beams that must sustain the structure of any enduring society.

Abraham was a man of major and universal insight and influence. He is the human hero of a divine drama, a strange, mystic figure who proves to be the file-leader of the highest religious conception and response man has manifested in reaction to God's impress upon him. His faith made him, not merely the sheik of a tribe nor the originator of a significant race, but the spiritual patriarch of humanity, the ancestor of many peoples, "the father of believers" through the ages. It was logical and is vitally significant that Paul found in this man the prototype of the Christian way of salvation.

The prophet of the second book of Isaiah was lifted to the summits of insight into the ways of God in history. He was permitted to look upon the draft of the purpose and the blueprints of the plan by which the peoples of the world are controlled and judged by the God of all the earth and all the ages. Isaiah and Paul are counterparts in the two Testaments. The apostle on his own independent basis and out of his own experience but amplifies the prophet, both were gripped and guided by the same cosmic concept, the same insight into history, the same faith in the sufficiency of the righteous and invincible grace of the One God.

Paul revered Abraham and interpreted him in the wider context of the universal gospel. The principle which Abraham held in a quietistic faith and with a foreshadowing hope Paul embodied in an activistic program for realization of the working of God in Christ, aggressively reconciling the world unto himself. What Abraham saw in the forward shining of a beam of light down coming centuries Paul beheld in the surpassing light of the glory of God shining in the face of Jesus Christ.

In Ephesians the whole content of the revelation of God through history and in redemption is summarized in condensed outline, so freighted with infinite meaning and so comprehensive of the meaning of the Christian fact and movement in history as to make it transcendent in the midst of all the marvels and the glories of the sacred Scriptures, the supreme monograph of all time. In it we are awed with "the glory of God in the Church and in Christ Jesus throughout all generations of the age of the ages." Its theme throughout is the glory of the Christian movement in the Christian Church viewed as the progressive life of God in Christ reconciling the world unto himself.

PAUL THE INTERPRETER

That Paul is the author of this writing is here assumed with little question and with no misgiving. For the interpretation of the book, its human authorship would make no ultimate, indeed, no really significant difference. Nor did Paul take any personal pride in his production; he was only an instrument. What he saw he reported and applied. While he frankly regards his understanding of the mind of God, working his will on the cosmic scale and in the full processes of history, to be nothing short of discerning what had through all previous ages been undiscovered, this was no discovery of his. By revelation it was made known unto him. Nor was it for himself. He was but the transmitter of God's intention in his Christ. His "understanding of the mystery of the Christ" was a grace of God committed to him on its way to mankind. It was a "secret" hid from all possibility of rationalizing discovery. Already as he announced it, it was revelation shared by all apostles and prophets, and it was to be shared by all men. That was the very purpose of its revelation.

Jesus had accepted the fact that God's great secret of his way in the world was "hid from the wise and understanding but was discernible for the childlike mind waiting to be taught" (Matt. 11:25). Paul knew that once the heart's eyes had been opened (1:16), believing men could know the center of God's meaning for the world and of the meaning of man for God. God had made known his secret intention in order that his plan might come to realization through the work of the gospel and by the working in men of his mighty power. "The secret of the Lord is with them that fear him" (Psalm 25:14), and to his "friends" Jesus opened up all the plan which the Father had made known to him (John 15:15).

Throughout the Epistle the apostle keeps steadily the viewpoint of God, and with reverent courage unfolds God's "plan of the ages" without apology and without question. While he discloses his firm belief that he is thinking God's thoughts after him on the scale of infinite ideas and purposes, there is no word of pride. He seems here to have been carried beyond his great experience of "the third heaven" (2 Cor. 12) when he heard words beyond the power or privilege of man to utter. That was at the time a very personal experience for him.

Now, many years later, he can forget himself and write down, for all to know, the very mind of God. He has come to this experience through many experiences. Paul has seen this divine "secret" of God work the most radical changes in men, seen it creating a new order of life by the power of God unto salvation, in Jew and Gentile, and in many races, cultures, religions, and degrees of intelligence. He has come to see that in his hands are spiritual weapons capable of casting down the fortresses of human wisdom. He has seen God through his gospel casting down the rationalistic philosophies and every high structure of knowledge that opposes the knowledge of God. He is able to capture and bring into the service of Christ every thought system and to avenge all disobedience to God in the measure in which the Christians shall be obedient in the gospel (2 Cor. 10:3-6). In these twenty years he has interpreted his secret from God in many situations, and through them all he has been led into ever deepening and broadening understanding of his revelation.

He has written many letters to individuals, to churches and groups of churches, to guide them in applying the truth of the Christ to the multiplex and multiform situations, conditions, and problems that confront the Christian movement as it grows in a world that is without God. He has had to cope with all the depravities of human nature as he led his brethren in Christ in their struggles with social sins and pagan ideals. In all this he matured his thinking and was led by the Spirit to integrate his insights into a unified philosophy of the Christ and Christianity.

PAUL'S DOCTRINAL TRILOGY

Christianity has its basic, constructive principles. The gospel is not a systematic theology nor, least of all, a system of philosophy, ethics, or science. But, as the gospel of God-in-Christ, it reveals a principle and a way of life and a vital power which demand thought formulation. Christianity is a gospel of life. Its life flows out of the all-comprehensive Life, which it proclaims as having been made concrete in one life in which God stands revealed and in which he works in history. If the gospel works as life, its life effects must be explained in their relation to the function of The Life. Christianity began without any express theology. Its effective working occasioned and made imperative reasoned statement of its central ideas, teachings, doctrines. Experience is first. Experience stimulates and guides the reverent reason as it formulates the Christian view of the world.

Paul's mind was led to give form to the central constitutive truths and forces which were working in human life and producing a mighty movement of regeneration and reconstruction. These truths for Paul centered in three vital and comprehensive doctrines—explanations of the nature, the scope, and the end of the Christian movement. Each of these is the theme of an "epistle." They rise in an expansive scale.

In Galatians he defines *the Christian way of salvation.* The necessity for this lay in confusion as to the relation between faith and works and as to the significance of these in relation. The importance of clear definition at this point was accentuated and aggravated by the campaign of some Jewish Christians to hold the nascent Christianity within the Hebrew tradition and system. The ceremonial system was for the Jewish mind in all its details "ordained of God" and essential to true religion. Hence it must be accepted as the groundwork for the new faith. The new faith was only the completing of the old, giving it vitality and appeal; but it must include all the forms of the old and be conformed to them.

As culminating in Jesus these forces found larger meaning and new power. For such Jewish believers there was one covenant, and only those within the covenant relation to God could enjoy his favor. The privileges of the covenant could be extended, but its forms must be accepted by all who would claim its salvation. Paul saw with deepest conviction that this view involved fatally erroneous concepts of God and of man, and made impossible the hope of a universal gospel and of the glory of God in human history.

These Judaizers undertook to rescue the Christian churches, including those produced in the pagan world by the ministries of Paul and his associates, from what for their thinking were the serious, if not fatal, defects of a religion which entirely omitted the Jewish system as such. Paul, on his part, felt bound to defend his Gentile converts, to save Christianity from the blight of formalism, ceremonialism, and sacramentalism, and to free it for its universal, spiritual function and destiny. There is a modern movement of Jews to recapture Jesus and to interpret him in terms of Judaism.

The root of the Christian gospel was to be found in direct approach of the individual soul to God through Jesus Christ and in the individual experience of union with God by the work of the Holy Spirit in man. A man is saved by God alone through the faith of the Son of God. He is thus free for, and constrained to, ethical expression of the new life and to fellowship with all of like precious faith in all godly living. "In Jesus Christ neither circumcision availeth any thing, nor uncircumcision; but faith which worketh by [working through] love" (Gal. 5:6); and all who have this experience through the Spirit by faith are in continuous expectancy of the righteousness of which their faith gives them the hope (5:5). This teaching Paul urges with all emphasis and completeness in Galatians.

In Romans, Paul takes a wider range. Holding steadily and emphatically to his exposition of the Christian way of salvation as in Galatians, he now goes on to outline *the Christian concept of righteousness.* Faith salvation inaugurates the highest possible demand and supplies the utmost divine energy for ethical living, individual and social. The man whose faith has accepted God's gift of justification is thereby committed to the conquest of sin at all cost and to "perfecting holiness in the fear of God." (The exact phrase is from 2 Cor. 7:1; but see Rom. 6:1-11; 12: 1ff., etc.) He is still keenly conscious of the conflict of teaching between Jews and such Christians as see with him.

Paul is under necessity also to satisfy his own mind about his new faith in its relation to his well-grounded belief in the "election of Israel" and his acceptance of their basic religious experience and teaching, none of which he believed he was surrendering or ignoring.

He must also think of Christian righteousness in relation to the universality of the gospel and of the race-wide objective of the reign of God in righteousness. In varying forms the erroneous ideas of formal and ceremonial requirements corrupted the concepts of religion in converts who came from all the existing systems, whose errors were certainly not less antagonistic to Christian truth than were the Jewish perversions of God's revelations to them. Paul was concerned to make central in thought the character of God, his righteousness, his holiness, his consistent integrity—"truth" is Paul's word. By contrast man's nature and its expression in ideas and in conduct is black with depravity and abundant in sins. God's love alone is equal to finding a way to rescue this man and fit him into God's righteousness.

With amazing cogency Paul binds all these interests into a condensed, closely integrated unity. Romans is his most logically ordered writing. It has through the centuries exercised the most powerful influence on Christian theology. Paul meant it as the exposition of the basis for a truly ethical religion. For him an effective religion must be thoroughly and passionately ethical, and it can be so only if based on sound and secure conviction as to God—theology; and on realistic understanding of man—anthropology.

Yet even in Romans, Paul does not reach his fullest statement of the Christian faith. He had all the ideas implicit, but he was not yet ready to expound and enforce as a high challenge to all believers the eternal grounds and the universal scope of the concept of righteousness which the gospel involves. For the exposition of the righteousness demanded by the holy, universal God and provided for man by his grace, Romans is sufficient. But for the working of this salvation and its righteousness in the entire history of the world and for its ultimate goal, this book is concerned only for the aspect of it involved in the problem of "the election of Israel" and the relation of this to Gentile inclusion.

His immediate purpose in Romans would have restrained Paul from following up the implications of many of his ideas, even if his own mind had been ready for this. In Romans, however, he had the heart of the Christian message. He would not be able to drop the great matter there. He must continue to reflect, to expand, to develop his own insights and their bearings. During four years of mostly unanticipated experiences his thought matured. His imprisonment in Caesarea and in Rome helped in different ways his preparation for his supreme statement. All that he had seen in experience, observation, and revelation came to be summed up in his thinking and in his adoration of God for the transcendent wisdom, grace, and glory in the expression of his nature in Christ and in the Church,* which for Paul is the continuance and the perfecting of the Christ.

In Ephesians he outlines *the meaning of the Christian calling.* This he does in the wide consciousness that Christianity needs to be understood in common terms by all believers in all sections of

---

*NOTE.—The word "church" as used throughout this discussion is capitalized or lower cased according to the author's interpretation of its particular meaning as applied to all believers as a spiritual entity or to different Christian groups or organizations.

the world in which it has gained its following. He also deeply knew that the Christian salvation was for all the world and that its comprehending Church must be universal. He was strongly determined also that its essential truth and experience must be preserved uncorrupted, else its value would be vitiated, its mission limited, and its unity rendered impossible.

All these features had emerged in one or more of Paul's writings. They were also, in varying measure, the concern of other leaders of the Christian movement. These considerations weighed heavily in the Jerusalem Conference (Acts 15). Paul felt himself chosen by Christ through the Holy Spirit to teach and defend these principles and to put them into the inner structure of Christian consciousness and into the institutional agency of the religion. For these principles he had suffered. For them he was ready to give his life.

To the Galatians, Paul had told how he had contended uncompromisingly at Jerusalem "that the truth of the gospel might continue with you"; and how at Antioch he resisted Cephas to the face because he led others, even including Barnabas, into hypocritical compromising in a way that jeopardized the integrity of the gospel and the unity of the Church (Gal. 2).

In the Corinthian correspondence he had humiliated himself in personal defense against many charges lest their minds should be corrupted from the simplicity and the purity that is toward the Christ (2 Cor. 11:3). And the factions in the Corinthian church were an intolerable affliction to his soul because they divided the Christ and tended to destroy his very body (1 Cor. 1:10-13; 3:4-9, 16, 21-23; 11:18ff., etc.).

Paul's persistence, against the advice and pleading of his most trusted friends, in going to Jerusalem at the close of his third period of missionary extension work is to be explained on the ground that the integrity of the gospel of salvation by grace through faith was still not secure; and, more definitely, because he was convinced that the threat of sectional, sectarian (denominational) division of Christianity was still strong and imminent. To him this was intolerable. It would mean the failure of the whole Christian movement. He must make his utmost effort to prevent this at whatever cost to himself. If the breach, always potential, should become actual and definite, there would be two religions claiming Jesus as the Christ; and neither could save the world and justify the sacrifice or fulfil the hope of Jesus.

A Jewish Christian church could never become universal because it would perpetuate racial arrogance and exclusiveness and would externalize the relation of God and man. Thus it would fail to reach the inner springs of life and personality and would lose its ethical quality. Being religiously and socially sectarian, it could not represent the one God nor reconcile all sorts of men both to God and to one another. And this two-dimensioned reconciliation must be the aim and the spirit of Christianity. Anything less is less than the religion of Jesus Christ.

Nor would a free Gentile Christianity represent God-in-Christ. Besides keeping alive the divisive racial consciousness, such a Christianity would lack rootage in the history of God's revelations and experiences with men. Without this historical continuity of God's approach to man, any religion must prove ineffective as a universal faith, fellowship, and ethical community.

All this Paul saw. And Jerusalem was still the field for seeking unity in the simplicity of the gospel, which alone could free it and keep it free for its universal meaning and mission. So to Jerusalem he would go, not knowing the things that should befall him there, save that in every city the Holy Spirit was testifying to him that bonds and afflictions were waiting for him. His own life meant nothing to him in comparison with bringing to completion the course of his administration function (διακονίαν) received from the Lord Jesus, to bear complete witness to the gospel of the grace of God (Acts 20:22-24). Nothing short of an unshakable conviction of necessity laid upon him to meet a supreme need would have led Paul to go forward against the repeated warnings which to a less independent soul would have had the finality of divine prohibition.

For not only did the Holy Spirit testify unto him in every city on his way from Corinth to Ephesus that bonds and afflictions were awaiting him (Acts 20:23); but at Tyre the disciples said to Paul through the Spirit that he should not set foot in

Jerusalem (21:4), and at Caesarea Agabus from Jerusalem met the apostle's party and by a dramatic pantomime gave a last warning. "Taking Paul's girdle, he bound his own feet and hands and said, Thus saith the Holy Spirit, the man whose is this girdle, shall the Jews in Jerusalem thus bind, and shall deliver him into Gentile hands" (21:10-11). All Paul's associates and friends were naturally convinced that it was his duty to surrender his plan. He answered, "Why are you weeping and crushing my heart? for on my part I am prepared not only to be bound but even to die there in Jerusalem in behalf of the name of the Lord Jesus."

Such determination and persistence grew out of the powerful conviction that the integrity and the life of the Christian movement were involved. The non-Christian Jews were determined to destroy any movement that claimed rootage in their religion and race and that appropriated their promises, their history, and their messianic hopes, and yet violated their rigid monotheism by centering their whole movement around the claim for their Christ of full sonship to God. They were set on rescuing from this blasphemous sect all Jews who had been drawn into it, or else on excising them definitely from the Jewish body.

Even the majority of Christian Jews retained their legalistic, ceremonial consciousness in a degree that endangered their sole reliance on faith in Christ Jesus and complete loyalty to him as God in saviourhood. As the first followers of the Christ, and as the necessary link in the continuity of God's grace through the redemptive history, these Jewish Christians must not be permitted to fall away from grace (Gal. 5:1-6). They must neither be reabsorbed in Judaism nor constitute themselves as a race-sacramental Christianity. They must not become a sect of either Judaism or Christianity. To avert this, Paul was ready to die. To labor for the unity and the simplicity of the Christian gospel and its churches, he would at all hazards go on to Jerusalem.

What befell him there is well known. Thus for four and a half years of imprisonment, with many and varied experiences and contacts, he had occasion to elaborate, to think through, to plumb to the depths his course, to criticise his convictions, to elaborate his insights and their implications and applications. He could—and could not but—review again his theology and philosophy as he had done in the three years in Arabia at the beginning of his Christian career (Acts 9:1-31; Gal. 1:15-24).

All these experiences and all this reflection, in the fellowship of the Spirit, prepared Paul by the latter part of his period of imprisonment to undertake the comprehensive statement of the meaning of Christianity. He may very well have written it in the last months or weeks of his stay in Rome. If, as is much more than possible, he had a period of two to four years between two prison experiences in Rome, he could have written it at some point of his ministry in the interim. Ephesus itself is not wholly out of consideration. And if it was written there, after first being spoken and then elaborated, this would account for one of the most difficult phenomena for the scholars: the entire omission of personal salutations or references in the document.

THE FULL CHRISTIAN SUMMARY

All who have given careful study to the Epistle agree that it is at once the most comprehensive, the most complete, the most incisive and creative of all the New Testament writings. It is beyond all praise, while it evokes most reverent and grateful appreciation. The philosophy of the Christian religion finds here its ultimate principles. Christian theology has no fundamental teaching that is omitted here, and the teachings are here held in balance such as is possible only when integrated in an architectonic concept which combines all elements in a natural relationship. Christian ethics find here their source and sanction, their aim and end, their persuasion and their power. Personal morality and social ethics are made interdependent and imperative, combined as aspects of life in the family of God.

Lidgett finds that "the Epistle to the Ephesians conveys St. Paul's final message to the Christian Church as to Christ, His work, and life in Him." When studied in relation to all the other writings of the New Testament, Lidgett further says: "It will then take its rightful place as the consummate and most comprehensive statement which even the New Testament contains of the meaning of the Christian religion, blending as nowhere else its evangelical, spiritual, moral, universal elements. It is certainly the final statement of Pauline theology." For him it is "not merely . . . the crown and climax of the Pauline theology, but of the New Testament as a whole."

While Goodspeed is so enamored of his hypothesis that the book is by a "great unknown" second-century editorial collector as to be certain that he has made its Pauline authorship absurdly impossible, he agrees still with all the scholars as to its supreme value. He even places its worth beyond Paul's discernment and ability—that of Goodspeed's Paul. Its "main tenor" Goodspeed finds in "the great jubilation over the worth of the Christian religion." The threefold purpose of this "Greek" compiler was: (1) "to set forth the transcendent value of the Christian faith for a generation of Greek Christians in danger of forgetting it"; (2) "to rally the scattered churches to a sense of their essential solidarity"—"a demand for Christian unity in the face of the sects"; (3) "a commendation of the collected Pauline letters to Christians everywhere."

Goodspeed's elaborate (he rightly says it is not exhaustive) tabulation of parallels between Ephesians and Paul's other epistles ("the nine letters usually recognized as genuine writings of Paul") is highly valuable for any detailed study of Ephesians. "Hardly a line of Ephesians is unaffected by those letters, in ideas if not in language, and every one of those letters has made some contribution to Ephesians" (p. 29). Goodspeed's hypothetical author-editor was so completely Pauline and so thoroughly Pauline as to have introduced into his compendium nothing at all alien to Paul in ideas or expression, and to have combined into a unity all of Paul's essentially Christian ideas from every one of his writings. "The writer must have been definitely holding himself to the materials of the nine letters." Paul would have been under no such artificial constraint and restraint. Those ideas had become so definitely the material of his Christian thought and he had so often placed them in his various communications as to make it wholly natural for him to use here, without effort and often without being aware of it, the terms that appear in his other epistles.

Lidgett has made a highly valuable comparison of the ideas and thought forms of Paul in Ephesians with those of John 14-17; First Epistle of John, and First Epistle of Peter (pp. 3-11). Abbott (*International Critical Commentary*) has compared language and thought of Ephesians and 1 Peter, and less fully pointed out parallelisms between this Epistle and Hebrews, the Apocalypse, and the Gospel of John, all of which he holds were later than Ephesians and may have been influenced by it (Introduction, pp. 24-29).

The marvels of spiritual insight, of ethical earnestness, of thought that dares use the categories of the infinite understanding, the emotional depths, that all belong only to men who are "beside themselves"—ecstatic—because of the sense of being used as instruments of God's revelation, found in all these writings impel us to worshipful reverence. Somehow, in Ephesians we see the possibility of the fulfilment of Paul's "striving in behalf of all who have not seen his face in the flesh, that our hearts may be encouraged as they are knit together in love and come into all the richness of full assurance of understanding so as to know the very mystery of God, which is Christ, in whom are hidden all the treasures of wisdom and knowledge" (Col. 2:1-3).

Subject and Major Emphases

An epistle does not require one subject. Usually it will not be organized about a single idea. Its purpose and nature will involve a series of topics, sometimes not logically closely related. In the case of Ephesians it is agreed by all students that it is not truly an epistle. It is, as we have seen, a treatise, as distinctly a unified treatise as is Romans; and among Paul's epistles, only Romans is properly comparable to it in this respect. Romans is, and is best understood as, the orderly development of the theme, "Christian Righteousness." Even the excursus into the problem of the Jews and their rejection of the Christian gospel (chaps. 9-11) is introduced and discussed in relation to the general proposition stated, from Habakkuk, in 2:4. "The just [man] shall live by his faith" (Rom. 1:17).

It is proper and desirable to find the writer's subject, if there is one. The expositors, for the most part, have not assigned a subject. The very perfection of the work of relating all the basic ideas and doctrines of the Christian faith in a closely knit outline makes it as unnecessary as it is difficult to select one concept as the constitutive principle for the whole. All Christian doctrines are interrelated and constitute a symmetrical whole. If any one of the major concepts is laid hold on and explicated, it is found to involve all the rest. Select any one of the major threads of its texture and draw it forth, and it will be found to draw along all the rest.

Any one of half a dozen, and more, subjects may be selected from the Epistle and all the rest logically integrated about it as central. It has a number of major emphases. Which is primary among them will be largely a matter of subjective choice of the expositor. Paul probably did have one idea which was central for him. But you could have set Paul off from any one of several starting points and then have followed him through the whole circle of Christian truth and experience. All the gems were on one string. Begin where you will, the sequence will complete the circle.

Lidgett begins with the doxology of 3:20-21, surely an alpine point in the great chain of primary Christian concepts. He selects as his subject "The Glory of God in Christ Jesus." In doing this, however, he omits part of the apostle's idea. Paul said "in the Church and in Christ Jesus." But with this as the guiding theme, Lidgett does give a well-integrated development of all the major themes of the Epistle. Yet one feels that it is Lidgett's, not Paul's framework. It is a modern pattern of the materials found in the original composition, not Paul's pattern. Other themes have been suggested. It is now suggested that Paul indicates what his own lead topic was. He would probably have had no special quarrel with any one of a dozen arrangements of his materials.

The Epistle is so often divided at 4:1 into "doctrinal" and "practical" sections as to lead us to that point to look for a unifying subject. One feels very sure Paul would never have consented to any division of his teaching into "doctrinal" and "practical" sections. He drew no such sharp distinction, as most expositors do, between these two aspects of truth and experience. It is a vicious distinction, dividing what cannot be put asunder without serious results for genuine religion. If doctrine is not practical—and practiced—it is unreal, delusive, and useless. If experience and conduct are not integral with truth, they are lacking in meaning and reality. Besides Jesus, no one has ever seen and said this more clearly and forcefully than Paul. Religion needs nothing more than to escape this distinction and the delusions that it engenders. It is a major source of confusion and weakness in Christian history and practice. As a matter of fact, we shall see that Paul does not leave even what theologians call "doctrine" at 4:1. So far as that transition may be allowed as having any validity, it is at 4:17 that he enters upon the "practical." But we need always to keep in mind that he made no such classification of his teaching.

Up to this point his approach was from the standpoint of

exposition and interpretation of experience of the truth; from this point it proceeds from the standpoint of application, living the truth. But the truth is always at hand and is interpreted in conduct experience. To this point we are led to see our experience from God's angle, yet all the way as God expressing himself in and in relation to man. From this point man and men are finding their life and meaning in response to God, to God as now with and working within them, not as having completed some plan and defined some purpose which is now given over to man to do what he will and may with them. All the way we have God and man in living encounter for the good of man, for the glory of God.

At 4:1 Paul manifests a transition in his own center of gravity, so to say. He does not leave behind for an instant the course of his exposition. He does go on with challenge and exhortation to human response. His form of statement shows how definitely he holds the two standpoints in unity. By a threefold use of the Greek root καλ (English, "call"), and by the use of the logical connective "therefore" (οὖν) he seems to suggest his own subject of the entire discussion and his sense of the integral relation of what goes before and what follows. We can set forth his play on this root syllable (καλ) by translating thus: "I *call you along* (call-along you), therefore, I, Paul the prisoner, in the Lord, to conduct-your-life worthily of the *calling,* with (or in relation to) which you *were called.*" This triple use of the word "call" can only have been intentional and significant. Paul's formative and informing subject, therefore, is *"The Christian Calling."* With this subject, and in logical adjustment to it of all parts of the "argument," we can unfold the ideas and follow the movement of the entire discussion. In this way we can feel fairly secure in the belief that we are going along with the apostle as he unfolds the source, the content, the meaning, and the appeal of the Christian calling. He is saying: "Here is what Christianity is; here is why it is; here is what it means to God, and how it means this to God; here is what it may mean to humanity and what it does mean for human history, and for the eternal purpose of the God of the ages, the God of the cosmic order and process."

Our outline will modestly undertake to unfold the mind of

Paul as he makes his way in outlining "God-in-Christ reconciling the world unto himself" and glorifying himself in "the Church which is the Body of the Christ" as Redeemer and Creator of a new humanity. But, first, we must call attention to some of the great constitutive features which control the thought and define its progress.

1. The very first fact to impress the reader, and the most powerful impression as he continues, is that *the entire book starts and proceeds from the God standpoint.* He is the subject of all the action, the source of all the experience. His glorification is the end of all the process of the transcendent and all-comprehensive cosmic and redeeming enterprise outlined herein. He is "over all, and in all, and through all" (4:6). This had long been Paul's starting point and the limitless limitation of all his thinking and striving. God was all the time at hand and active for Paul even while God was always far beyond him.

In Romans, in awed reverence, he had exclaimed of the fathomless wealth of both the wisdom and the knowledge of God, whose judgments and ways are beyond our following through to full comprehension. "For out from him, and by means of him, and with him as their end are all things. To him be the glory into (all) the ages. Amen" (11:33, 36).

Already in 1 Corinthians (15:20-26) he had looked at the full work of the Christ unto its consummation, when he will turn over the completely won kingdom to God even his Father. The Father had in projection "put all things in subjection under the feet of the Son." Now, with every enemy finally overcome, "then even the Son himself will take his place in the order, subjected to him who had put all things under his control, so that the (one) God may be all in all" (v. 28). The Son will be absolute as the Head of the perfectly ordered system, yet in relation to the Absolute God of all will hold himself within the order which he has perfected, unto the glory of his Father God.

Paul never overlooks this God-over-all reference, not even when he is realizing most fully the supreme place of Jesus Christ in the economy of redemption, as the creative factor in human history and cosmic process. In Colossians, written in close relation to Ephesians, where we have the sublimest passage in exaltation of the Christ, it is still kept in mind that in all things the Christ has his pre-eminence "because it seemed good (to the infinite God) for all the fulness (of the vital universe) to abide in him and that through him all things upon the earth and in the heavens, should be brought into full reconciliation unto God" (1:3-20, N. B. 18-20).

The focal point in all the thought about God in the Epistle is his "glory." All the book revolves about that. No part of it can be understood if that is lost sight of. God's character and purpose are glorious. All things are made to demonstrate "the glory of his grace." His plan, his hope, his inheritance, his power—all express his glory and evoke his glorification. The cosmos and the creation, his gospel and his salvation, his redeemed family, the temple of a unified humanity, his infinite love—all things glorify him through the reverent recognition by discerning souls of God's infinite wisdom, love, and grace. The apex of the book is in the doxology in 3:20-21. This doxology in its sublime conception is not surpassed in the most exalted songs of universal praise in the Apocalypse. "Now unto him that is able to do exceeding abundantly above all that we ask or think, according to the power that worketh in us, unto him be glory in the Church and in Christ Jesus throughout all ages, world without end. Amen."

2. Equally outstanding and important is *the experiential nature of the book*. The God whom it glorifies is no metaphysical abstract deity; no logical or ethical presupposition. He is no philosophically necessary Ground of Being, no theological construct. He is living, acting, loving, always instant Person. Paul would never try to catalogue the "attributes" of God and distinguish between the "communicable" and the "incommunicable." He does not think of omnipresence, omniscience, omnipotence. God is everywhere present, all-knowing and active in all action. We have here no abstract or theoretical description of purpose and plan which we ascribe to God. It is a report on the mind and moving of God as seen by one who looks on with awe and reverence, who is taken into the confidence of the working God,

and who is even given a share in the working. It may indeed be quantitatively an infinitesimal share, but qualitatively ours is a part infinitely important.

From the first word right on the plan is seen as the direct activity of God as he operates within us. The personal sphere of God's activity is always before Paul. With Paul we see God at work, and we are let into the secrets of what he is doing. We are ourselves in part, an infinitely significant part, the material with which and within which God is working.

Paul presents the Christian experience not objectively as something which is possible and is commended; he discusses it as an experience of his readers. It is explanation of what we are experiencing. An especially impressive disclosure of this intensely experiential nature of the discussion is the fact that repeatedly the apostle begins a statement in the second person and then, apparently but probably not actually, unconsciously he falls into the first person. Examples will be seen in 1:12-14, 18-19; 2:1-4; 8-10; 3:19-20; 5:2: "*ye* were sealed", "which is an earnest of *our* being inherited"; "that *ye* may know; . . . the greatness of his power toward *us*"; "*ye* were dead; . . .but God; . . . for his great love wherewith he loved *us*"; "*ye* have been saved; . . . *we* are his workmanship"; "that *ye* might be filled; . . . according to the power that worketh in *us*"; "Christ . . . loved *you* and hath given himself for *us*." These transitions emphasize the experiential consciousness that is characteristic of the entire discussion.

The thrill of this immediacy of the active God arouses the reverent awe and stirs the eager response at every turn as we follow through the description of the work of God in the process of redemption. We are made to share the apostle's humble exuberance as we feel the grip of God's purpose and power upon us and the amazing grasp of his hand of love upon all that we are called upon to lay hold on with our hands. God is indeed working in us to will and to achieve what his perfect vision sees to be good. In that fellowship with God in working we are constrained to "work through to completion" not our personal salvation alone, but the whole divine undertaking with us in our sphere. This word from the somewhat earlier Philippian letter from the Roman imprisonment might well serve as a starting point for the appeal in all the Ephesian letter for loyal response to God in faithful striving unto righteousness. For God and man are linked in thought and experience through the whole of it.

Such is the experience one is invited to share in the description of the way of God in his work in man, through the beloved Son, and by the action of the sanctifying Spirit. Paul begins, after the salutation, with an outline of the purpose and plan of God in the Christian calling, 1:3-13. This is presented not abstractly nor objectively. It is not the setting out of a logical or theological basis upon which to construct a scheme of theoretical history and to make an appeal for human response. Here is not a preliminary "look-in" on the "eternal council chamber of the Godhead" to discover a chart for theological and ecclesiastical form and work. From the first word to the end of the document we are led to realize God at work in ourselves. By defining this experience, we discover and amplify our discernment of the divine plan and his limitless purpose.

Thus man is given transcendent meaning and worth, dignity and glory, in that he is made the willing instrumentality and agency of the life-activity of God.

In chapter 2 the Christian experience is described as human experience of divine action. Man's spiritual regeneration, his re-creation, is part and parcel of one comprehensive activity of God in producing a new creation. Here, then, is the love of God in action seen in the grace that rescues and saves. The social experience of this love-grace is the new humanity which becomes the holy dwelling place of God.

In chapter 3, where we have the wider, even the widest, aspects of the Christian calling, it is still God in action producing human experience in fullest measure. God's many-sided wisdom is being made manifest by what he is doing and getting done through the Church. He is achieving his own fulness in the full redemption of humanity. Man accepts and responds under the motive of love in which he is rooted and grounded (v. 17). In chapter 2, God moves in love to create the man who can love. In chapter 4 the love motive is expressly seen, both in God and in man, in the one great activity of growing a perfect Body of the Christ (v. 16).

As this body of the redeemed yield themselves up to the Christ, they come to understand the dimensions of the incomprehensible love of God. Thus they are corporately rounded out into all the fulness of God. In this prayer we are brought to the daring thought that in the experience of the called God is having, extending, and completing his own experience—"up to all the fulness of God." His ability to achieve beyond all the capacity of human asking or aspiration lies in his own energy already at work and continuously working in us.

3. *Ethical emphasis is inherent in the entire concept of the Christian calling.* In chapter 4, where Christian man is called upon to respond worthily to his calling, we do not find balancing, complementary action of God and of man. It is not distinctly human reaction to divine action, nor is it independent human response to the call of God. God is still acting, but acting now within man. We see and experience God in us reacting to his own action for us and in our behalf. Here, in Christians, and especially in the Church Body, we have divine behavior in human conduct. We have the action of man when God uses humanity as the sphere of his own reaction to action of his own in the realm of man, as man. Here man becomes, because invited to become, enabled to become, rejoicing to become, voluntarily and aggressively united with God, in what is for God a supreme undertaking. The Christian man must express in his living the nature of God. The Christian society must seek to embody on earth the relations and standards that obtain in heaven. We are to become imitators of God as his beloved offspring and to order our lives in practical grace in the spirit of the love of the Christ (4:32-5:2).

Man now works with a holy earnestness and complete dedication, because he is aware that God within him and he within God in Christ have a common enterprise. This is mystical experience but also is deepest reality. Now in ethical social expression the mystical becomes divinely practical.

As the motive of God in all this glorious undertaking is his love, so the capacity and the possibility of Christians for serving

God in his fulfilling must rest in their being "rooted and grounded in love," love being the inspiration of their comprehending their calling of God in Christ Jesus and responding to it. In 4:16 this all-achieving love is both God's and man's, man's because he has been taken up into God's love; and by this love the Body is building itself up. That superhuman humanity which God requires he gives and in the giving achieves it as objective reality. Here man is challenged to become, is enabled to become, and rejoices to become consciously and aggressively united with God as God's own objective response to his subjective intention.

This work of man as he is now linked up with God is in a realm of sin and evil, in a social order—and disorder—that is "alienated from the life of God, because of the ignorance that is in them, because of the hardening of their heart" (4:18; cf. Rom. 1:18-32). God is working out in his redeemed a new era in the midst of "this present evil age" (Gal. 4:4). Hence the love of God is working through social love, which he creates and develops by his Spirit in "the called," to produce a new order of society, a new world. This divine love is the motivation of all the Christian experience prescribed and described in the last three chapters of Ephesians, which deal with the practice of the Christian calling in human life and in all human relations. Here the divine love becomes concrete and individual. It is all the more divine love as it becomes constraining love in redeemed human beings.

Here divine experience becomes human experience, and human experience becomes godly. This is the ground conception and implication of all the ethical exposition and appeal in chapters 4-6. The exalted ideals and standards of Christian ethics are based in the unified relation of man in God so that man's conduct becomes God's action. Since we live in God, God acts in us. All in the Church of the Redeemer are members of his body. He acts in our conduct. "Be ye therefore perfect, even as your Father which is in heaven is perfect" (Matt. 5:48).

4. *The exaltation of Jesus Christ* is impressive throughout Ephesians. This is nowhere in this Epistle lifted out in a single section for very special emphasis as in Colossians 1:15-20. It is

assumed and the place of the Christ in every relation and interrelation between man and God is integral in the exposition. Christ never substitutes God nor becomes independent of God in any function or act; neither does God appear in this Epistle as acting toward or in behalf of man except "in Christ."

The Christ is always the channel of God's every response in man to God. This is true also in Colossians and Philippians. It is a normal form of Pauline thought. We experience "God in Christ"; and it is "through him" that we all "have our access in one Spirit unto the Father." In the passage in Colossians which gives to Christ "the preeminence in all things," his supreme dignity is as the "Son of God's love" into whose kingdom the Father has transferred us. In that passage he is designated by no other name or title than "the Son."

In the salutation to Ephesians, Paul is "the apostle of Christ Jesus by specific act of the Father"; the greeting is to those who are "faithful in Christ Jesus"; grace and peace are invoked "from God our Father, and from the Lord Jesus Christ."

God's blessings have come to us "in Christ," we have been chosen for sonship "through Jesus Christ," and God's free grace "was bestowed on us in the Beloved." All things are to be "summed up in Christ." It was "in the Christ" that the Jews had been "foreordained" and "in him" that the Gentiles are included in salvation.

All these examples from the first fourteen verses are characteristic of the entire presentation. Christ is the all in all for the Christian salvation and for the Christian movement. When God raised him from the dead, he caused him to sit at his right hand, superior to all orders of rule and reign, order and administration, for the present and for the coming age as well; while for the Church he is "head over all things." He is in all respects filling to the full all God's programs in the process of the entire world order. In Christ all things were created: in him all are re-created. All Christian relations to God and to men, and all activities within these relations, are "in Christ," "in the Lord," "in Christ Jesus."

The question of the Trinity arises here. In the descriptive argument of the Epistle usually there is functional and logical arrangement of the Persons in the Deity, and these are stated without metaphysical explanation, and this method is maintained with consistency. Wherever the connection naturally permits, the Three who constitute the Trinity are named as if on parity, but never with any express statement as to their mutual relationship or gradation in rank. The logical order is, however, always preserved, Father, Son, Spirit. The prepositions, if any, are always appropriate and consistent for the function of each Person within their relationship. In a word, the book reflects no formal metaphysical concern and no systematic theology consciousness. This is in accord with the usual New Testament approach and method. The Trinity was discerned through experience and accepted on the basis of functional analysis of the Christian experience. This process of discovering and handling the fact of the Trinity gives the doctrine firmer ground in reason than if it were a metaphysical construct justified by the fact that it constitutes a convincing frame for defining the total Christian experience.

This purely incidental emphasis on the Trinity of the Christian God appears repeatedly in the Epistle and leaves no room for doubt of its integral implication in earliest Christian thought. That it seems to have been arrived at with such unanimity of agreement without controversy and without recorded deliberation is one of the truly remarkable facts in the history of Chistian thought. Only later, when theology became dominant over experience, do we find controversies.

Paul introduces himself as "an apostle of Christ Jesus through an act of the will of God." Then he joins "God our Father" with "the Lord Jesus Christ" as the source of "grace and peace." In the first paragraph the processes of universal history and of redemptive history come from God the Father through Jesus Christ, while the saved are "sealed with the Holy

Spirit" (1:3-13). "The Father of glory" and the supremely exalted Christ are inseparably linked in the filling of all things (1:14-23). Individual regeneration and all the content of salvation are wrought in men by God exercising "his grace in kindness upon us in Christ Jesus" (2:1-10). In creating a new humanity, God reconciles the opposing racial fragments by slaying their enmity through the atonement of the cross; and thus "through him (Christ) we have our access, both groups of us in one Spirit unto the Father" (2:18). So in the building of the "holy temple" of redeemed humanity, Christ Jesus is himself "the chief corner stone" and the temple "in the Lord" is occupied by "God in the Spirit" (2:20-22).

The "mystery" of the universal Christ and of his gospel is made known in "the grace of God" "by revelation" unto Paul, as unto all God's "holy apostles and prophets in the Spirit." "The unsearchable riches of the Christ" "hidden from the (previous) ages in God" are now the stewardship of the Church, which the Spirit makes "strong for indwelling by the Christ," so that through "the love of the Christ" God may achieve all his "fulness" in the fulfilled Church (3:2-5, 8-9, 16-19).

The unity of the Church is "the unity of the Spirit." Its one body is vitalized and harmonized by the "one Spirit," in the interest of the "one Lord," all in final reference to the "one God and Father of all" (4:3-6).

Christians are to be careful to "grieve not the Holy Spirit of God," in whom we were "sealed unto the day of redemption," but to "be kind one to another, tenderhearted, relating yourselves to one another in the principle of grace, just as God also was gracious to you" (4:30-32). The principles of living and the conduct of Christians in the heathen society are to be determined by the consideration that they belong to "the kingdom of Christ and of God." When in danger of depression and failure, they are to "be filled with the Spirit," who will give them victorious hymns and "Spirit-given odes" with which to sustain themselves and keep them "giving thanks for all things in the name of our Lord Jesus Christ to the Father-God," all the while "subjecting themselves to one another in the fear of Christ" (5:5, 18-21).

For the Christians' warfare "God's armor" will make us "strong in the Lord," while we use "the sword of the Spirit," constantly "praying in the Spirit."

These examples from all parts of the Epistle reveal the apostle formulating experience and thought in terms of "God in three persons, blessed Trinity," not as theological dogma but as the sustaining energy and atmosphere of the Christian soul. God moves in Christ, who works through the Holy Spirit.

This all-comprehensive mediation of the Christ between God and men, in both directions, is a chief feature in all the epistles. Also, in all Paul's writings, whatever Christians do is "in the Lord," in every relation. And this Trinitarian interpretation of God in action, so constantly the characteristic form of Pauline thought, is in full harmony with the reported experience and teaching of Jesus and with the other New Testament writings. Never argued, never formally stated, this is a most significant fact.

5. *The Church is a major concept* in the structure of the Epistle. To be sure, the term occurs in only three of the six chapters. Yet the concept is to the fore throughout, so much so that the entire contents may easily be logically integrated about this concept as if it were the subject of the whole, without doing any violence to Paul's thought and without rearranging any of the material.

The Church in Ephesians and in Colossians is the spiritual Body of the Christ, constituted of all who are children of God through the calling of God and by their "faith in the Lord Jesus." This Church is conceived as organic with the Christ, his Body in the world, in the process of redemption, in the unfolding of history. In this sense the Church is not organized, has no human head or headship. It is, as such and as a whole, no more concrete or visible than the Christ himself is concrete and visible in the sense world. As individual members of the Church Body, Christians are of course concrete, visible units in the general social order. Much of the Epistle is devoted to the principles and practices which must characterize their lives as members of Christ in the midst of the non-Christian society and world.

It is assumed in a general way that, as members of the Body of Christ, Christians are members of an organized church. This is taken for granted but never formally so stated. Indeed, in this Epistle an organized church is never once named nor explicitly referred to. Paul's other writings do speak of the churches, some of them quite definitely, and First Corinthians elaborately. In every city, including its socio-economic and political community, all believers were united in the fellowship of an organized church, which was the co-operative Christian community, the obvious, tangible expression, in its social context, of the Church, the "new humanity" which God was creating in Christ Jesus. These city-community churches were not within the New Testament institutionally integrated in any common organization or any grouping beyond their own organization. These visible, institutional Christian fellowships were of vast importance as the means of developing the experience and understanding of individual Christians; as the working agencies of the gospel; as the social expression of the Christian faith and of the ideals and principles of the kingdom of heaven. In First Corinthians we have interpretation and guidance for this organized church and an extensive exhibition of the problems which such a church must meet and solve as a distinctive institution in the midst of a secular society. These problems appear in less specific and detailed form in Ephesians, but are here dealt with in the context of the total Church as the Body of the Christ.

Here the Church is first brought forward as the Body of the Christ who is its "Head over all things." As such it is ideally and by design "the fulness of him that filleth all things in all respects" (1:20-22). From this Epistle and others we know that this means that God expresses his entire purpose and activity in creation and in redemption, and in the historic process in the Christ. "In him dwelleth all the fulness of Deity in bodily form" (Col. 2:9; cf. 1:19); and therefore "in him ye are made full" (Col. 2:10). This is Paul's way of saying, with

John (1:1-18), that Jesus Christ is the all-inclusive and all-exclusive Word of God and that all that men become by his grace they get by receiving of his fulness. The unique thing in Paul is that he links the Church up with the Christ as an essential counterpart and extension of the Christ in his filling to fulness the will and work of God.

Under other figures the Church is exalted and destined for highest glorification in chapter 2. In chapter 3 it becomes the growing embodiment of the "mystery of the Christ" and as such, according to divine purpose, it makes known to all realms and constituted orders the many-sided wisdom of God (10-11).

In chapter 4:1-16, employing the word "Body," the apostle carries the Church to the utmost conceivable limit of relation to the Christ. From this point he proceeds to indicate how the members of this Body of the Christ are to express his mind and will both within the Body and in the complicated relations of human life.

It is in 5:22-33, that the term "Church" is used repeatedly—six times—setting forth the relations of Christ and his Church as ideal and inspiration for the relationship of husband and wife in the family. Of all this we shall see more fully in the detailed exposition. The point here is that the Church is here conceived as the most exalted, holy, and glorious unity of human beings conceivable. It is constituted of human beings called in the foreknowledge and purpose of the Father love of God; redeemed by the beloved Son through the blood of his cross; made alive from death in sin by the Spirit of power; developed and wrought into a holy unity by the one Spirit. "The Christ loved the Church" in prospect and in process, "and gave himself up for her; that he might sanctify her," "so that he might set the Church alongside himself in her glory, free from spot or wrinkle or any such defect, but according to his provision glorious and without blemish." Men are, of course, incorporated into this Church only by the grace of God in regeneration; and all who are thus regenerated become in that experience members of this Body of the Christ.

The organized, visible, working church unit is ideally and

properly the local, regional, social expression, counterpart, and embodiment of this universal spiritual Church. Membership in it is for all who have the experience of grace. It is voluntarily entered as the home and habitat of the redeemed soul; the nurturing environment of the growing spiritual life; the family fellowship of all into whom the spirit of sonship has come teaching them to call God Father; the organic instrument by which each one is wrought into the harmony of the Body of the Christ, its Head; the agency for serving the saving Lord in the witness of his gospel; and the ethical society by which he brings in the kingdom of God. Every man who experiences the grace of God is called into the fellowship of "the saints in Christ Jesus." If one has been made alive in the Spirit, he walks by the Spirit into the fellowship of a church, because he is a member of the Church. It would be wholly incongruous to think of the Holy Spirit, who is creating and perfecting the universal spiritual Body of the Christ, as regenerating an individual and leaving him outside a definite church fellowship. The course of any son of God by faith in Christ is voluntary. At the same time, he acts "in the Spirit." Being in the Spirit must include being in fellowship of the saints in a church. (See further discussion of the Church Pp. 43-79.)

6. The ultimate reference for every element in the elaboration of the Christian calling being God, and the fact that the final objective of the Christian movement in all its elements and operations is the glory of God, involves the choice by God of all the means and all the instruments that enter into the process. This means that the *Christian doctrine of election* is inherent in the unfolding interpretation of the work of God in history. Nor is this left to inference. While the substantive term, election, is not found in this Epistle—as it is indeed not frequent in the Scriptures—still the thought is utilized at every turn and is definitely affirmed, even though in subsidiary clauses only.

That God has a "plan by which he constructs and directs the ages" is an essential element in the statement of the universality of the gospel and of the Christians' stewardship of the universal gospel (3:1-11). That God "chose us in the Christ before the founding of the cosmic order" is at the heart of the very opening paragraph (v. 4). The Jews "were made a heritage of God, having been foreordained according to the plan of him who effects all things according to the counsel of his will" (1:11). Those who come to be adopted into sonship through Jesus Christ had been "foreordained" unto this gracious experience (1:5). It was because of the great love God had for us while we were still dead in trespasses and sins that God made us alive, even including us by anticipation when he was raising the Christ from the grave.

Then, to emphasize that the sole initiative and work for our salvation is in God, it is emphatically said that this experience is God's gift to us, not of ourselves in any sense (2:1-10). There is no need to establish this point nor to argue it; it is one of the most obvious and presumptive ideas in all Paul's thinking. And yet it is not pre-eminently any contribution of Paul's, for it is in the very fiber of the Scriptures and is necessary to the biblical conception of God. God who knows, cares, has power, and has purpose must have plan and plans. He chooses means and instruments. This is election.

What greatly needs to be pointed out and insisted upon is the setting in which Paul puts the teaching as to God's choice and foreordination. There is no teaching of the Christian faith which has been more misconceived and more perverted than "the doctrine of election." The misconception of this doctrine hinders the work of Christianity and vitiates its theology as does no other perversion, unless it be the humanistic definition of the person of Jesus Christ. The error does not at all lie in the facts of God's purposes, plans, foreknowledge, and foreordaining of all things "according to the good pleasure of his will." No God without purpose and plan, without knowledge of all he is undertaking, or who is lacking power to carry it out would meet the conditions of any world that could exist, of any history that could endure and progress. The producing and making actual a spiritual and ethical realm out of the human material which we are could only be of grace. It must be the work of God. Nor could a competent God be an experimenter, learning by trial and error and readjustment. The reading of the King James Version of Acts 15:18 (where the Greek text is uncertain and its meaning not clear) expresses a central conviction of the Christian faith: "Known unto God are all his works from the beginning of the world." Certainly Paul had no question that "all things are of God" (2 Cor. 5:18). This is a positive ground of his entire discussion of the Christian calling, and it bulks large in the declarations and the assumptions of all the Bible.

In the Bible election is introduced and discussed, so far as discussed at all, uniformly as the choice by God of men, nations, institutions, religious groups to participate in or to be used in his purpose and his plans. His choice is made not primarily from the standpoint of its advantage to the elect. This choice on the part of God does usually involve and result in great advantage to the chosen, but by no means always. Cyrus was elect, and his selection is set forth with elaboration and great emphasis. He is the one man who is called Jehovah's Messiah. (See Isa. 44:24 to 45:17.) Paul (Rom. 9:14) illustrates the sovereignty of divine choice in the carrying on of his purpose by the saying about Pharaoh (Ex. 9:16): "For this very purpose did I raise thee up, that I might show in thee my power, and that my name might be published abroad in the earth."

Taking the principle of election as primarily for the benefit of the elect, and conceiving of it as in all cases meaning choice for salvation and as terminating in the elect person or persons, has been the starting point for many evils in the Christian churches. Here is the great mistake in the interpretation and application of the doctrine, antinomianism. The repudiating of human responsibility, indifference to Christian obligation to the lost, to heathen, to social evils have all had this error as one of their main roots. Protestantism neglected the missionary obligation for nearly three centuries because of depraved indifference, which was not only excused but justified as a virtue of faith. This attitude was supported by appeal to false interpretations of election. The truth of the security of the believer was turned into practical falsehood by the ignorant way of construing belief so that God is irrevocably committed to the eternal blessedness of all whom he has elected unto salvation.

Many passages of Scripture have been misconstrued and perverted in meaning by being employed as proof texts for an erroneous doctrine of election. The most glaring example is the famous, popular word of Romans 8:29-30, where the succession of operations of God in his redeeming grace are so wonderfully set forth. "For whom he foreknew, he also foreordained" is read as if it were a complete sentence. Or it is completed, not as Paul completed it, but by adding in thought if not in words "unto eternal salvation," or "unto heavenly bliss." Paul wrote "foreordained to be conformed to the image of his Son, that he might be the firstborn among many brethren." Foreordained, that is, to the achievement, in God's grace, of the character of Jesus. The whole passage is part of the elaboration of the insistence that the man of faith is irrevocably committed to the conquest of sin and to godliness in character and life (chaps. 6-8).

The climax of perversion of the doctrine of election is in the denial of the purpose and power of God in Christ Jesus to save the world through the gospel. Those who deny this then commit themselves to a "dispensationalism" that postpones the effective proclamation of the gospel to another "age" and consigns the vast majority of humanity to hopeless sin and evil. Even in "the age to come" these interpreters depend on force to overcome evil and to bring in the kingdom of heaven. Accordingly they not only reject the application of the gospel to the social order but account it presumption even to desire to do so. Not a few of those who magnify this conception of election account themselves as peculiarly honoring God and as having peculiar insight into his eternal counsels.

The opening paragraph of Ephesians illustrates well Paul's concept of election and may serve to contrast it with the perversion of the truth. Here we read how God "hath blessed us in the Christ . . . even as he chose us in him before the foundation of the world." In love he had "foreordained us unto adoption as sons through Jesus Christ." The primary objective of all this is strongly emphasized by keeping it before us at every stage of the outline. He chose us "to be holy and blameless before him"; foreordained us for sonship "unto him"; and it was all "according to the good pleasure of his will"; and to the end of "the praise of the glory of his grace" (4-6). Again, our redemption through the blood of the Beloved was looking toward "a stewardship of the fulness of the times" for carrying out God's purpose, "to the end that we should be unto the praise of his glory" (7, 11-12). And the Holy Spirit marks believers as belonging to God while he is working out complete possession of what he has claimed as his own, "unto the praise of his glory" (13-14).

The point to note here is, not that these believers were not chosen for and endowed with personal salvation. They were, and "the elect" are usually those "who are to be heirs of salvation" (Heb. 1:14). The point is that the saved are "elect" not merely as individuals destined to eternal personal salvation but are chosen and called to participate in the plan of salvation which God is working through Jesus Christ to save the world, to found and perfect his kingdom, to glorify himself in human history. The chosen ones are foreordained to take part in "the integrating of all things, in heaven and earth into a harmonious whole in the Christ" (1:10). We are chosen for service, for stewardship, saved to serve in the plan of saving the world. This is the emphasis in the whole of Ephesians, in all Paul's writings, in all the New Testament, in all the Bible.

Jesus did not call men first of all to follow him into heaven but to enter into the kingdom of heaven, into its service and sacrifice, its righteousness and redemption. This way of thinking of election and foreordination is absolutely necessary if we are to follow the thought in Ephesians, and it will affect our understanding of the Epistle at all stages.

7. *Other concepts* besides those emphasized here are involved in the Epistle, but those discussed here are constitutive and structural and must guide us in studying the Book. We shall find here "the clue to history," the basal principles of the Christian view of the world. These principles are assumed and used in the course of the discussion; they cannot be taken as its subject throughout, nor used as parts of the structural plan of

the treatise. All the essential Christian doctrines are to be found here, but some of them are introduced incidentally because they are inevitable.

Regeneration, for example, essential as it is, is not expounded but introduced as an accepted essential. Here are the principles for an ideal social order, but no explicit social gospel. In no sense is the Epistle a sociological tract; yet it involves the principles of a righteous society. Paul employs some of the key terms of the mystery religions and of the gnostic interpretations of the world process, but he is not constructing a polemic against those erroneous systems nor an apologetic adjustment of Christian doctrine to them with the direct purpose of winning proselytes from them. He gives no outline of these religions or of their teachings. He does not even refer to any of them by name. Yet his references and his laying hold on their special technical terms do mark out the line for a proper apologetic in this field. He appropriates some of their terminology because he can thereby at once make Christian truth clearer and disclose the insufficiency and error of the "mysteries" and of the hypotheses of these cults. We shall need to take account of these as we come to them in the course of exposition.

The Church as Continuing Incarnation of Christ

In following Paul's thought concerning the Church through our Epistle, and especially in chapters 1:22-23; 2:20-21; 3:14-21; 4:11-16, we found the Church so intimately and so essentially related to the Christ and to his meaning in history as to constitute his growing self-realization in the process of accomplishing the ends of his incarnation. The Church is his growing Body, so that in it he is himself growing into maturity, "unto the measure of the stature of the fulness of the Christ." Certainly that concept cannot be applied to the Christ as the eternal Son of God, to his essential being and personality as such. It can only be understood of the Son in his incarnation experience and function. The Son is the Christ—the Messiah, the Anointed—only in his experience and function in history. The Word of God in world process "became flesh and dwelt among us men" to make concrete and practically effective in empirical history his work of producing sons of God (John 1:1-14; Phil. 2:5-11). This is "the incarnation." It was an event in time, the experience of a particular time, place, and situation. Yet it was not just an event in time, an experience of a particular time. As such it would be a powerful demonstration of divine interest in man, a powerful persuasive influence over man. But it would be outside man and would act upon him as argument and influence, as appeal and inspiration, as promise and hope. That is not what the gospel brings to us.

In the incarnation the Christ revealed himself as the creative and redemptive power of God in humanity. All the time he had been "in the world" which was "made by him" and "was his own." In becoming flesh he entered into human life, not for a moment or for a few brief years of sojourn, but once for all. He took upon himself our nature to become its constructive and reconstructive factor. The Church became once for all the embodiment of the Christ in human experience and history.

On Pentecost, according to his plan and promise, the Holy Spirit sanctified the Church to be his growing Body. Thereby the Christ is no longer only with his people but is within them. His incarnation has appropriated them for its extension. This in essence, if not in exact form, is Paul's meaning in his interpretation of the Church in the "Prison Epistles."

The Hebrew Christian experience and history are the product of following the call of eternity implanted in the human heart, under the prophetic interpretation of God, first of all as Immanuel (Isa. 7:14), and then as God-in-Christ reconciling the world unto himself (2 Cor. 5:19). Through the Christ, God reveals that he has purposed a stewardship of history by which he carries humanity forward toward purposed fulfilment which consists in harmonizing all things in all the universe under the headship of the Christ (Eph. 1:10; Col. 1:16-20; Phil. 2:5-11, etc.). The Church is that growing fulfilment.

Christianity is the religion of the Christ. It originates with him, is conditioned in relation to him, is the interpretation of him, is the reception and appropriation of him. It is his self-realization in and by means of the working of redeeming grace of which he is the complete embodiment. All that God is and means and does is found in him in concrete, "bodily," expression and action.

Now in the New Testament the working, the achievement of this redeeming spiritually and ethically creative Christ is embodied, expressed, measurably and progressively realized in the Church. Jesus the Christ is the surpeme fact of history, the founder and the fountain of the Christian movement. Christ Jesus is the supreme factor in the making of history as he is also in the entire creative process of the universe. The *cosmic* Christ is historically identifiable in Jesus, revealer of the eternal God. The *cosmic* Christ is manifest and made relative in Jesus. He does not begin in the birth of Jesus nor end in the death of Jesus, nor even in his ascension. He was before all things; he continues through all time and beyond time.

One must take instructive account of the use of the term

"manifest" in relation to the Christ. It is a feature in the thought of him all through the New Testament. It was the *Logos,* who from the beginning was the active counterpart of the creating God, in whom, as Jesus Christ, grace and truth came into active operation in empirical history. Because no one ever at any time has seen God, the One who exists as Son in the Father's bosom, that One, as "uniquely begotten God," brings God out into human apprehension.

This was not the origination of a person or of an activity, but it was the manifestation of the deepest reality and fact of God in relation to humanity (John 1:18).

The nature of God and his attitude toward men were potentially manifested to all men in physical nature (Rom. 1:19); and God's righteousness was not originated but was manifested, in law and prophets, and supremely and ultimately "by his grace through the redemption that is in Christ Jesus whom God put forward as a mercy-meeting-point ("propitiation") through faith in his blood; and this became a demonstration-in-action (ἔνδειξιν) of his righteousness. This demonstration of righteousness in active forgiveness enables God to go on justifying any who come unto God through the faith of Jesus, without any violation of the divine principle of justice (Rom. 3:24-26).

Thus it is that "now, once-for-all, he hath made his appearance at the climax (ἐπὶ συντέλειᾳ) of the ages with the designed end of putting away sin through his sacrifice.... So also the Christ will-be-seen (ὀφθήσεται) a second time . . . by those who are awaiting him unto salvation" (Heb. 9:26-28). "Ye know that he was manifested to take away sins," and "to this end was the Son of God manifested, that he might destroy the works of the devil" (1 John 3:5-8). Thus "the love of God was manifested (made evident) in us in this, that he, God, sent his only begotten Son into the world (κόσμον) in order that we might live through him" (1 John 4:9).

There is no need to accumulate citations. The characteristic representation of the Scriptures is that God's character, purpose, and work are not from time to time, in great epochal events, originated or essentially modified; the great acts and events are only relative "comings," demonstrations, manifestations, not radical originations. The Christ does not *become,* nor in the strict sense does he *come;* he *appears,* just as God makes his presence manifest.

The English translations have reflected and perpetuated an erroneous form of thinking by frequent use of "come" or "came" where the Greek text has (ἐπιφάνεια) "appearance." The writer is strongly of the conviction that in important connections the second coming of the Lord is indicated in the English translations where the incarnation "coming" (appearance) was intended. One example is at 2 Timothy 4:1,8. To understand this to refer to his appearing in his incarnation fits better in both connections here. So also *parousia* (παρουσία) is limited by being rendered "coming." Its etymological sense of concurrent presence is basic, even when "coming" may be useful for specific defining. Especially suggestive is 2 Thessalonians 2:8, where, whenever "the lawless one" shall be disclosed, the Lord will destroy him by the breath of his mouth and render him ineffective by the *epiphany* of his *parousia*—i.e., by the manifesting of his concurrent presence.

The point of all this preliminary discussion in this connection is to affirm that the incarnation is not, and in the New Testament is not presented as, simply a single historic event in the course of God's redeeming activity. Rather it is an event which reveals that activity, which makes it concrete and which can have meaning and validity as the effective force and factor in the "gospel of the grace of God which hath appeared bringing salvation to all men" (Tit. 2:11) only if it is a living, continuing fact. In Jesus, the Christ is with us; the *Logos* has "taken up residence among us" (John 1:14). In some way in vital presence and power his incarnation experience and meaning must continue, expand, and develop. For if it is a fact, this fact is the most significant and determinative event in human history and the most meaningful factor in the working of the purpose of God in history.

Luke, in his twofold Gospel, Luke-Acts, presents the incarnation meaning in primary terms. That he represents Paul, as also the widely discerned apostolic apprehension, may be assumed. For him "the gospel of the glory of the blessed God" comes in two complementary, essential forms, or parts. In the first he gives the account of God incarnate in a Person; in the second he tells of God incorporate in a community of new life, the body of believing witnesses who continue the presence, purpose, and power of the Christ. "The former treatise" tells of what Jesus "began both to do and to teach until the day in which he was received up," after he had provided for his continued doing and teaching when he had been "received up." This provision he made by "giving commandment through the Holy Spirit unto the apostles [messengers] whom he had chosen," and who were "charged not to depart from Jerusalem" until they had received the fulfilment of "the promise of the Father, which ye have heard from me." This fulfilment would come in their being "baptized in the Holy Spirit." In this experience of baptism in the Holy Spirit, the Christ would continue not only with but, far more significantly *within,* his disciples. In deep spiritual reality his disciples would become his Body, his Church.

The unity of incarnation and incorporation, in the Luke-Acts way of conceiving, is strongly emphasized in the fact that the author attributes both experiential events to the Holy Spirit as working cause; and in the further fact that the Spirit continues his presence and power both in the event and in the ongoing life of the Christ in all experiences and work of Jesus, and in the Church in its experiences and work in the name of Jesus. Luke, above all the Gospels, associates the Holy Spirit with Jesus from his generation to his giving of the resurrection day commission. In a very real and significant sense this dual Gospel is the Gospel of Jesus and the Holy Spirit.

This way of thinking suggests influence of the very striking, if little noticed, word of Isaiah 48:16. Here Jehovah's servant, in the first instance Cyrus, but any personal instrument in a crisis of history, is made to explain himself by saying: "And now the Lord Jehovah hath sent me and his Spirit." We are reminded again of Isaiah 59:21 where Jehovah's "covenant," looking to universal redemption and glory, is made "with the Messiah and his seed"; and this redemption is to be effected by sending his Spirit "upon Messiah and his seed and his seed's seed from henceforth, even forever." With the Spirit upon them, "Jehovah's word is also in the mouth of Messiah and of his seed." This union of the Spirit and the Servant in the solution of any crisis and in every case of redemption becomes the supreme fact in the supreme Servant and in his "seed" who constitute his Church. In the Gospel the Holy Spirit originates the human Jesus; in Acts he embodies himself in the Church as continuing Christ.

Acts is written as the record of the working of the Holy Spirit in the followers of Jesus as they interpret, extend, confirm, and develop his life as the Son of God become the Son of man. It is best described as "the Gospel of the Holy Spirit in the Church," and it can be correctly analyzed and understood only under this concept. It should be clear that for Luke the Christ and the Church constitute one event, and that the Christ continues his presence among men in the Church.

It is, however, important for the understanding of the Church concept to note here that Luke uses the term, and the specific concept of the church, sparingly, and that with a single exception it connotes only the local Christian group, and as a group rather than as institution. The exception is, of course (9:31) where, after Saul's persecutions were at end, "the church throughout all Judaea and Galilee and Samaria had peace, going-on-in-process-of-upbuilding, and, walking in the fear of the Lord and in the inspiration [comfort] of the Holy Spirit, kept-multiplying." It should be obvious that Luke is here thinking of "the church throughout all Judaea and Galilee" as spiritual entity and fellowship body and not as institution or organization. Even when, as in all other examples, he uses the term to indicate specifically a local group of Christians, he seems to think not of institution or organization but of a local fellowship of disciples, for whom organization was functional.

The Gospel of John, never employing the term church at all, discloses Jesus as eagerly and intensively depending upon his self-extension and self-perpetuation in his followers for the success and justification of his ideal and his sacrifice. And in this Gospel the spiritual oneness and continuity between him and his following constitute one of the formative concepts of the entire book.

That this early Christian understanding and experience was due to Jesus, alone can explain the part the conception plays in this Gospel. And it runs through John's first epistle also. The love of God which "sent his Son *to be* the Saviour of the world" "is perfected in the midst of us" who "confess that Jesus is God's Son." "In us God abides and we abide in God," "because just as that One (incarnate Love) is, so too are we in this world." This strong declaration of 1 John 4:12-17 attests the belief and experience of the Church at the end of the first century and declares it in terms of the words of Jesus in the "upper room" plans and assurance with which he faced his crucifixion (John 13-17).

The Gospel gives as the ground need for the incarnation man's empirical incapacity to see God unless he is made manifest. In the Epistle the Christian following is explained on exactly the same ground: "No man hath beheld God at any time"; but "if we love one another, God remains in us; and his love is brought to completion in us" (4:12). Begun in the Christ *Logos,* continued in the Church *Logos.*

In the upper room (and at Gethsemane) we enter the deepest consciousness of Jesus. Here he identifies those who believe on him truly and are his own, as constituting a spiritual and a practical unity with himself. His new commandment of love is to bind them in a unity that will convince "all men" (13:35). The great works which God has begun in him he will make greater through those that believe in him. He and they will be united in love and prayer with the Father. He will not leave them desolate; through the Holy Spirit they shall become aware of a unity wherein "I am in the Father and ye in me and I in you." Thus both Father and Son will have abiding presence in men who are loving and obedient (14:12-24).

Jesus and his followers are related as vine and branches. Out of this vital union comes all the fruit of the mission of salvation. He and his words will continue to live and function in them, his love will continue in them, his joy will be in them, and their joy will come to fulness in their common relation with him in the world (15). The Holy Spirit will make the followers mightily aware of the Christ present with and within them; will make them able to convict the world with respect of sin, of righteousness, of judgment; able to overcome the world (16).

It is in the final prayer with them (17) that Jesus goes all the way in identifying himself with "his own whom the Father has given him and whom he has won and held." They are to remain in the world for him, for, as the Father has sent him, so he sends them into the world. They must be made and kept in unity of love and purpose. Here is the unity of redeeming activity in a trinity of world approach: "The glory which thou hast given me I have given them, that they may be one, even as we are one: I in them, and thou in me, that they may be perfected into unity: that the world may know that thou didst send me, and thou didst love them even as thou didst love me." (Note the aorists).

Throughout chapter 16, as also in 14 and 15, the Trinity is Father, Son and Spirit (Paraclete). The three appear in the record repeatedly. Now in the prayer of 17 the Spirit is entirely omitted by name. Here the Trinity is Father, Son, Believers. No explanation of this change from Spirit to Believers is given in the text, but is it not evident? The Holy Spirit comes upon and resides within the believing group, and the world is convinced. Only as, but emphatically as, the believing group is infilled, empowered, embodied by the Holy Spirit in the Church does it become a member of the Trinity of the redeeming gospel. The Spirit remains the divine Person in the Godhead, but he functions for the redeeming work of the Godhead in the redeemed. To be the embodying of the Holy Spirit, to take his place in the tri-unity of grace in the world is a sobering and a sanctifying conception. Is it a reality?

It is through Paul that we have most fully developed the concept of the Church as the continuing presence and work of the Christ in history. Something of this appears in his earlier writings. It all comes to climax in Ephesians. In this book the apostle undertakes to interpret the meaning of Christianity as a movement, a force, and a factor in the history of the human race, in the divine plan and procedure in history, and even in the cosmic purpose and work of the God of all. Here he summarizes the ground of a compelling challenge to all Christians. As "the prisoner in the Lord" he "*calls-along*" all believers to "*order-our-lives in-a-way-worthy of the calling wherewith we were-called*" (4:1). The entire discussion moves about this central, architectonic concept. The two foci in his presentation of the activity of God in redemption are the Christ and the Church. These two are so intimately related as to be essentially interrelated and to constitute one entity.

Head and Body constitute one unit.

This is one of a number of thought patterns which Paul employs for conceiving and interpreting the work of God in human history, a history that for Paul, as for all the Bible, is redemptive history. Yet history is not in any limited sense exclusively redemptive. History is, and especially in Paul is conceived as, creative, constructive, progressive. Redemption is a necessary factor of cosmic process and of creative consummation, in which all human history is to reach its glorious goal in complete unification of all things under the headship of the Christ. Within his comprehensive, progressive, constructive work God included the human race.

The race as it is, is intractable material, "dead in trespasses and in sins" (Eph. 2:1-10, etc.); "alienated from the life of God, etc." (Eph. 4:17-19. Cf. Rom. 1:18-3:21). The "natural man" has "the mind of the flesh," which "is death," "is enmity against God," "not subject to the law of God, neither indeed can it be" (Rom. 8:1-11, etc.). Hence the Christian calling begins in redemption and proceeds with redemption always an essential factor in its process. The redeemed constitute an "elect," a "called-out group," hence *the Ekklesia,* the Church, which is Christ's Body in the midst of the world order and of the history-making process.

We have said that this is a thought pattern, one of several thought patterns. In Ephesians 2:11-22 we find at least five such thought patterns under which to conceive the Christian following and movement. (See Exposition section.)

All these thought patterns are suggestive illustrations and carry graphically a basic fact in the experience and the aim and the goal of Christianity. But none of them is, for Paul, comparable to his biological pattern. The vital relation between Christ and the Church is no mere thought pattern; it is mystical truth which can be expressed so vitally and so essentially under no other concept. This is the dominant and structural core of the Epistle and takes us to the most intimate and profound understanding of the value of Jesus Christ for history and for the glory of God in history.

After presenting the individual and social experience of all God's called, and seeking in the five thought patterns of the latter half of chapter 2 to indicate the nature of God's "product," "created in Christ Jesus," Paul comes a second time to pray (chap. 3). But before the prayer is an outline statement of God's deep and ultimate plan in the Christ ("the mystery of the Christ"). This "mystery" is that all races are equally in God's love and equally in his redeeming plan. By the stewardship of this plan through the gospel, God will, by means of the Church, demonstrate to the principalities and powers in the heavenly realms his many-sided wisdom. Thus here, the Church and the Christ are unitary in the making and in the carrying out of God's eternal purpose. They are complementary counterparts. The Christ creates his Church and continues his working in it.

Now the prayer (3:14-21). And we must keep in mind that it is a prayer for the Church. The plural pronouns are to be understood collectively, not distributively, in the first instance. You are to be made so strong by his Spirit coming into and working within you that the Christ may have in you—the Church—a place to dwell, a sphere to work in, an instrument of action. You will need to know the incomprehensible love of the Christ in its four dimensional reach. And all this because the Church ("you") is to be filled out to the entire fulness of God's redeeming purpose. This is in exact accord with the declaration of 1:22 that the Church is the full content of the Christ as he fully carries out all God's purpose. Hence, in the transcendent doxology of 3:20-21, God's glory throughout all generations of the age of the ages is to be realized "in the Church and in Christ Jesus."

Now for the Church's response, which must be worthy of the high calling (4:1-16). In meek and long-enduring love the Church, in all its members, must zealously guard its unity. There is a sevenfold ground for the plea of unity. Each member of the Church has from the ascended Lord his own gift in order that the Christ may fill all things. In this Church under specially functioning leadership all the saints are to minister toward building up the Body of Christ.

And here we come to the boldest, the most awesome, the most compelling phase of this biological challenge concerning the Christ and the Church. The thought is so daring, the concept so supernal as to cause us to halt and fear to follow. Indeed no interpreter has been found who dares to accept in full the clear meaning of the passage. All the saints are to give themselves to the building of the Body of Christ "until we all—corporately and collectively and unitedly—arrive at the unity of the faith and the accurate knowledge of God's Son, even, therein, unto a mature man,—(yes, let us dare follow through)—unto the measure of the stature of the fully realized Christ." From the perfect Head all the Body makes its increase unto building itself up in love. For in this process the Body is harmoniously framed and firmly integrated, through every joint drawing and transmitting its supply from the Head for the full functioning of each and every part.

Thus the perfect Head, through the growth of the Church, actuated by love, by means of his supply of grace, attains to the perfection of Head and Body, and becomes the fulfiller of all the fulness of God. He attains the measure of the stature of the full-grown Christ. The personal incarnation is continued in and finally to be perfected in the Church in which he has his incorporation.

It is important to ask what is the nature and what are the relations of his Church which is so intimately united with the Christ. We usually make a wrong approach here, because Christian history has largely thought of the Church as a divine institution, a powerful organization closely integrated and carefully administered and guarded. Jesus placed first importance on life. He produced a living organism, assigned it functions and proposed himself to continue with it, its sustaining life.

From his own nature, aims, methods, relations "in the days of his flesh," we may find our starting point and our touchstone. He was "in the world but not of the world," and he expressly affirmed this as his ideal and purpose for "his own who are in the world." He was not concerned with religious institutions as such. He would prevent them from restricting and perverting the freedom and responsibility of men in relation to God, from hindering spiritual values, reverence for God, the reign of God, the doing of the will of his Father on earth as it is done in heaven. He was tremendously and persistently, passionately concerned for a Kingdom; but his kingdom was not, is not, "of this world." He will have no kingdom and no institution such as would compete with the political, economic, and social institutions of men. He came from God and speaks to men as Son of God, and he came to men as Son of man, of humanity, not to any section of mankind, racial, national, or class section. All men are under the judgment of the universal God of every nation. All are judged by the standard of that oneness for which God created and providentially controls all divisions of the race, aiming always at the unity into which God calls them all through his Christ and through his Church.

Into this Church the Holy Spirit brings men by individual, personal regeneration, and they "all become children of God by faith in Christ Jesus." The nature of the Church must be understood from its relation to the Christ of God, and from the ideal union of the Christ and the Church in relation to the full intention and interest of God in the whole order of life and reality.

No one has grasped this central truth concerning Christ and the Church better nor expressed it more clearly than Dr. Salmond in *The Expositor's Greek Testament* in connection with Ephesians 1:23 (p. 281). There Paul indicates that he is dealing with a unique and supremely significant entity and relation: "The word σῶμα (*soma*) which passes readily from its literal meaning into the figurative sense of a *society,* a number of men constituting a social or ethical union (cf. Eph. 4:4), is frequently applied in the NT Epistles to the Church, with or without τοῦ χριστοῦ *(tou Christou),* as the mystical body of Christ, the fellowship of believers regarded as an organic, spiritual unity in a living relation of Christ, subject to Him, animated by Him, and having His power operating in it. The relation between Christ and the Church, therefore, is not an external relation, nor one simply of Superior and inferior, Sovereign and subject, but one of life and incorporation. The Church is not merely an institution ruled by Him as President, a Kingdom in which He is the Supreme Authority, or a vast company of men in moral sympathy with Him, but a Society which is in vital connection with Him, having the source of its life in Him, sustained and directed by His power, the instrument also by which He works .... The preceding sentence carries the idea of the *Church* far beyond the limited conception of a concrete institution or outward, visible organisation, and lifts us to the grander conception of a great spiritual fellowship, which is *one* under all varieties of external form and constitution in virtue of the presence of Christ's Spirit in it, and *catholic* as embracing all believers and existing wherever any such are found. It is the conception of the Church which pervades this Epistle (cf. iii. 10, 21; v. 23, 24, 25, 27, 29, 32). It appears again in similar terms in the sister Epistle (Col. i. 18, 24), and elsewhere in the varied phraseology of the 'royal priesthood' (1 Pet. ii. 9) and the 'Church of the Firstborn' (Heb. xii. 23). It is this supreme idea of the Church as a spiritual order the essence of which is a living relation to Christ, that receives further expression in the profound sentence with which the paragraph closes."

The Ephesian emphasis, after the vital, spiritual, experiential insistency in the expository discussion of the calling in the Church in chapters 1:3-4:16, is on the ethical quality and moral idealism and conduct of all members of the Body, in their mutual relations within the Body and within the normal, necessary social relations of life in the family and in the local church body. This moral and ethical idealism in behavior is urged in the personal conduct and especially in the social relations of the Christ community in the secular world. The local church community, just as the entire Church Body everywhere, must segregate itself morally and ethically from the heathen, secular world (4:17 to 5:21). There is no reference to the Church as an institution.

What is the relation of the Church and the churches?

It is to be understood, although it is never explicitly asserted in this Epistle—and that is important—that the Church is represented locally in an organized, functioning church. This local church is nowhere in the New Testament treated as a "part," "branch," or "unit" in any organized, catholic, ecumenical church. However one may interpret the fact in its significance for Christian history, it is a fact that in the New Testament there is no one general organized Christian body—no one visible institution of which the visible local bodies are member units. These local units are responsible to and under the administrative guidance of no central individual or group of any sort, anywhere. The local bodies are fellowships rather than institutions or branches of an institution. Their officers are functional rather than institutional. All Christians ("saints") are encouraged and earnestly exhorted to cultivate a sense of unity with and a unique "love for all the saints."

The Christian movement is one Church, but the churches are not under nor in one church in any outward, institutional sense. The universal Church is spiritual, and membership in it is given and accepted by spiritual experience of regeneration expressing itself in personal faith and committal. The local church, the only organized Christian body found in the New Testament, is constituted of such as have received the Word of the gospel and, impelled by the Holy Spirit, have associated themselves together as a fellowship of worship, a band of witnesses, an ethical community, "a colony of heaven," proclaiming the Word of God, practicing the ideals of the kingdom of God, and looking for the fulfilment of the promise of Christ's appearance "to take his great power and reign" (Rev. 7:15ff.). Only in 4:8-12 do we find mention of any who might be thought of as officers of this universal Church. The way in which they are introduced and the functions indicated by their titles do not suggest that they are officials of the Church as an institution. They are gifts of the ascended Lord "to men." The Church is not an institution nor an organization such as would call for officers or administrators. They are not officers in the Church, certainly not officials over it. By its very nature it would not, nor could have officials or offices in the institutional, organizational sense. A "hierarchy" or even an "order of the ministry" would be quite unthinkable in the Church so far as it appears in the New Testament. Of the four functional gifts here named, the first three have to do with the initiation of the gospel in new areas, with its extension and with giving it in each new area an established footing and the fitting understanding of the nature, relations, and work of the Christian body, within itself and in the social context, as also in relation to the full Christian enterprise.

First of all, we find "apostles," the Greek term, instead of which in evangelical vocabulary we have used the Latin word, "missionaries." They are the first bearers of the gospel in any area. Along with them went "prophets." Their function was, under immediate guidance of the Spirit, to interpret the will of Christ in any problem or situation requiring special guidance beyond ordinary human understanding. "Evangelists" are "bearers of the good news." The three examples of the use of the word "evangelist" in the New Testament (here, in Acts 21:8—and see chapter 8, and 2 Tim. 4:5) suggest that their special function was to carry the gospel to the suburban communities in the environs of the cosmopolitan center in which apostles and prophets had planted a church. They were thus, in our American terminology, community or "home" missionaries in connection with a central church. In the New Testament organized churches included in each case all Christians in a metropolitan center and its social and economic community. It would normally soon have numerous functioning subcenters, calling for a multiplicity of ministries and ministers. "Evangelists" developed these secondary centers.

The life and work of the over-all church body were supervised, developed, and directed by "pastor-teachers," who seem to have constituted a body of "elders" in every city-wide church. (Cf. Acts 14:23; 15:6; 16:4, etc.). The connectives in the Greek text clearly suggest one office with the two functions. To the one organized church group they give permanence, progress, order, and growth, instruction, and administration.

Yet the one church which is their immediate responsibility is not an isolated or spiritually complete entity. While they function in the churches, they do so in the consciousness of the Church. In them Church and church meet. If they lose sight of the Church, and function with only the church in their purview, the effect is to segregate and isolate the organized body from the spiritual Body and to hinder and limit its unity.

So far as Ephesians is concerned, we deal primarily with the Church as the total Christian movement. The leaders it lists are those who represent the movement as a whole. They receive their calling and conduct their functions under direct action and empowering of the Spirit, but in the spirit of the one Body and with a sense of interdependence. As the first three types of leaders succeed in gaining a group of believers, they lead them to constitute a church. The Lord in the Spirit provides the chief leaders for the local body, "pastor-teachers." The church now enters upon its career.

In 1 Corinthians 12-14 the organized church is discussed as the body of the Christ in that community. The body is created by the Holy Spirit through the power of the gospel. First of all, he causes each individual to accept Jesus as Lord. That is the common, initial, and essential "spiritual gift." "No one is able to say 'Lord Jesus' except in the Holy Spirit" (12:3). Starting from that experience, the Spirit bestows his many and varied "gifts" on all the members, as members of the one body and in its interest. Thus the church is made one, and in that community "is thus even the Christ" (v. 12 literally). In discussing this church, in Corinth, Paul lists "varieties of gifts," all "inspired by one and the same Spirit, who allots them to each one as he wills." Thus are produced, not "orders of officers," but "varieties of service," in "varieties of working," and all "for unified progress" (4-11).

In this list of gifts for this church, apostles (missionaries) and evangelists are not named. The prior work of these originators of the church is assumed. All the functions are named as ways of serving, no "officer" being mentioned. At verse 28, having finished with the matter of the interrelation of the members of this particluar church, the apostle turns to a more general view of the Christian movement to say that "in the Church," in general and as made concrete in the church, "God has set, first, apostles, second, prophets, third, teachers, and then" various other functions—named as functions, not as personnel in whom the functions find expression. The order, "first," "second," "third," and on is not here nor elsewhere in the New Testament presented from the standpoint of relative authority or even of dignity, but from the standpoint of the logical order of their ministry "in the furtherance of the gospel."

This understanding of the Church and the churches, and of the ministries within the churches, is borne out further by a similar discussion, with variations, in Romans 12. Here the list has immediate application to the church in Rome. Comparison of the two passages and of both with the list of four ministries in Ephesians 4 clearly indicates that Paul was not thinking at all of "orders in the ministry" but of ways of service in the gospel and in the churches which embody and promote the work of the gospel. Certainly no one can find in Paul any explicit support for any fixed and essential institutional "order" integrated around and administered in succession by a permanent authoritative "ministry." Every such claim is at most supported by inferential reading back into Paul some later system.

As we have seen, in the New Testament "The Church" connotes the spiritual Body of the redeemed. As such it never appears as an organized institution, comprehending all the churches, but these are everywhere autonomous local units.

During the second and third centuries, by a gradual process, the Church did come to be conceived, preponderantly, as a general institutional organization, comprehending, subordinating, and combining in outward union the churches. In the fourth century this Church attained power to punish nonconformity and to suppress all churches which did not accept incorporation into it. The concept of such a comprehensive Church has been the starting point of theoretical discussion and practical procedure of the majority of Christendom until our own day.

The development of European nationalism and of Protestantism, with the interaction of state and church, produced the concept of "Churches" in another sense, partly denominational and partly politically geographical. Lutheran, Reformed, etc.; and Anglican, German, etc., are examples. And these classifications overlap in German Lutheran, German Evangelical, Dutch Reformed, Swiss Reformed, etc. All these conceive the Church, with whatever limitations of national and confessional relation and tradition, as including, uniting, and supervising all the churches within a given area which become its jurisdiction.

All the way along, the counter concept which begins with and maintains the integrity and complete autonomy of the local church has persisted in spite of minority status, ridicule, repression, and persecution. When the Protestant Reformation arose, this conception of autonomous independence on the New Testament pattern was one of the forms of the movement. It gave promise of becoming powerful. It had some inherent weaknesses. It was vigorously antagonized by all the "Reformation Churches" and violently persecuted almost to extinction. In the last two or three centuries, chiefly in the United States but increasingly elsewhere, this type of church is commonly now designated congregationalism. It had its modern resurgence and expansion from the Independent movement in England. If we take the Church, as in the New Testament concept, to be the spiritual Body, it precedes the churches, logically and in experience. The churches are constituted of those who by regeneration of the Spirit have been introduced into the "new humanity" which is the Church. If we take the Church, as in the main stream of outward Christianity since the second century, to be the (or some) organized body incorporating and giving validity to the churches, we must face the fact that historically "the churches" preceded and made possible the Church, so understood, and that in turn it assumed priority and superiority over the churches. It supports and defends that superior status by a subtle and usually unconscious identification of the general organized Church with the spiritual Church of the original New Testament Christianity. In the New Testament no such comprehensive institutional Church can be found.

Outline

Painstaking effort has been made in this treatise to discover and to follow the forms of Paul's own thinking. This is not a modern outline of the material, intended to apply to current conditions the principles and teachings of the writing, but a sincere effort to reproduce the thought organization of the apostle as he composed it. Expositions will undertake modern applications in some practical measure. Here the humble ambition is to help the reader to see the working of Paul's own mind as he sought to set forth in condensed outline what was given to him as the deepest, widest, most comprehensive meaning of Christ Jesus and of his Church Body for the eternal purpose of God in human history. He thought of this meaning in its cosmic setting; in its unfolding of the religious and social history of the human race; in its progressive revealing of the nature and personal qualities of the God of grace and glory; in its possible value in justifying and glorifying God for the understanding and appreciation of the intelligent universe throughout eternal ages.

Yet Paul never left the earth nor lost himself in clouds of metaphysical speculation. He was always concerned for ethical interests and for the outcome in human behavior, in personal character and social attitudes, conduct, and institution. He was never more earnestly practical than when he was most profoundly metaphysical. He was never building an abstract system, a thought construct. Always he was seeking to set men and mankind in their true setting in God's plan of the ages and to cause them to experience conscious, living relation to the active redeeming work of God in Christ Jesus.

It is with that insight and conviction that this Outline seeks to give a moving picture of the apostle's mind as he dictates this terrifically condensed philosophy of the Christ in his Church fulfilling God's intention in history.

THE GLORY OF GOD IN THE CHRISTIAN CALLING

Salutation 1:1-2

I. THE GLORIOUS PURPOSE AND PROJECTION—Chapter 1

1. The calling presented from the standpoint of the Triune God, 3-14
   (1) God's eternal choice "for the praise of the glory of his grace," 3-6
   (2) God's elect have a stewardship of history through the redeeming Son "unto the praise of his glory," 7-12
   (3) All groups as they believe receive the sealing pledge of the Holy Spirit "unto the praise of his glory," 13-14
2. The concept of the calling described in a prayer that the redeemed may understand God's intention in their calling, 15-21
   (1) Praise for the called, 15-16
   (2) Prayer for their insight and understanding, 17-21
      a. That the Father would give them the Spirit of insight and revelation, 17
      b. That with open-hearted vision they might know their significance to God, 18-21
         (a) What is God's hope in calling us, 18a
         (b) What is God's wealth in the called, 18b
         (c) What is God's power for achieving his purpose in the called, 19-21
3. The calling to be realized in the relation of Christ and the Church in its fulfilling, 22-23
   (1) The supreme exaltation of the risen Christ, 22a
   (2) Christ the supreme Head of the Church, 22b
   (3) The Church the Fulness of the Fulfilling Christ, 23

II. THE GLORIOUS EXPERIENCE OF THE CALLED—Chapter 2

1. The new men created in Christ Jesus—individual experience, 1-10

(1) The dead material with which God must work, 1-3
(2) The life-giving experience of grace through faith, 4-6
(3) God's glory in his graciousness toward us, 7
(4) God's pre-provision for the life activity of the re-created, 8-10

2. The new humanity created by the blood of the cross—corporate experience, 11-22
   (1) Keep always in mind the contrast—then and now, 11-13
   (2) All divisive distinctions abolished and peace established, 14-16
   (3) Peace and unity preached in the name and by the work of the Trinity, 17-18
   (4) God in Christ through the Holy Spirit producing a new sort of humanity: one body, one human race, one family, one commonwealth, one architectural structure, one temple for spiritual occupation by God, 19-22

III. GOD'S PLAN OF THE AGES TO ISSUE IN UNIVERSAL GLORY THROUGH THE CHURCH—Chapter 3

1. Approach to prayer for the Church, 1
2. Explanation of "the mystery of the Christ," as preparation for the prayer, 2-13
   (1) Paul's stewardship of the universal gospel, 2
   (2) Paul's understanding of "the mystery of the Christ," 3-4
   (3) This long unrecognized mystery now God's open secret, 5
   (4) Terms of the mystery, 6
   (5) Paul's double function in relation to the mystery, 7-9
   (6) The Church the instrument of God's plan of the ages and the revealer of God's wisdom to the universe, 10-11
   (7) Paul's personal response to the plan of God in the the universal gospel, 12-13

3. The prayer for the glory of God in his Church, 14-19
   (1) The character in which God is here addressed, original, archetypal Father, 14-15
   (2) Three petitions, 16-19
      a. That the Church may be strengthened to be indwelt by the Christ, 16-17a, b
      b. That the saints may all together grasp the incomprehensible love of the Christ, 17c-19a
      c. That the Church may fully express the full intent of God, 19b
4. Glorious doxology, 20-21
   (1) Glory to the infinitely effective God, 20-21a
   (2) Glory in the Church and in Christ Jesus (as perfected Head and Body), 21b
   (3) Glory into all eternity, 21c
   (4) The Amen, 21d

IV. THE GLORIOUS CHALLENGE TO THE CHURCH AS THE PERFECTING BODY OF THE CHRIST—Chapter 4:1-16

1. The called called upon to prove worthy of the calling, 1
2. The spirit required for worthy response, 2-6
   (1) Full, humble committal of self in relation to other members of the Body of the Christ, 2
   (2) Active, unremitting zeal for perfect unity of the Body, 3-7
      a. Impelling forces for unity of the Spirit, 3
      b. Sevenfold ground of unity, 4-6
      c. Threefold relation of the One God, 6
3. Individual responsibility of each within the Body, 7
4. Gifts of the victorious Christ for the building and perfecting of his Body, 8-13
   (1) The right and the purpose of the Giver of all the gifts in the Church, 8-10
   (2) The functions of the gifts and the one determining end, 11-12a

(3) The constraining end and spirit for all the saints in the Body, 12b-13
(Note that verse 13 pivots two items in the outline)

5. Full co-operation of all for the glorious goal—the complete Body of the full-grown Christ, 13-16
(1) The transcendent goal which must enlist the unified co-operation of all, 13
(2) Hindrances to be met and mastered, 14
(3) Joining loyally in all things with the Head, 15-16
a. Being true to him, 15
b. Vital, effective dependence of every member on the supply of the Head, 16a, b
c. Faithful, harmonious, healthy functioning of every part, 16
d. Thus the Body builds itself in love, 16c

V. GLORY IN THE COMMUNITY OF THE CALLED—Chapters 4:17 to 6:9

1. A distinctive community within the order and the confusion of the world, 4:17-5:14
(1) Must be ethically and morally segregated from the "heathen" world, 4:17-24
a. Low ideals, standards, and conduct of the "heathen," 17-19
b. The Christian standard found in the truth of the Christ as demonstrated in the life of Jesus, 20-24
(2) The Christian body must live in mutual loyalty, love, and graciousness, 4:25-5:2
a. "Members of one another," must deal truly in all relations, 25
b. Contrasting attitudes and behavior indicated in basic relations, 26-31
c. The example of God and the sacrifice of the Christ in love inspire and impel to loving graciousness, 4:32-5:2
(3) Sexual morality must be carefully guarded, 5:3-14
a. All forms of such social sin utterly incongruous

with Christian ideals and impossible in the kingdom of the Christ and God, 3-5

b. Theories justifying or excusing sex sin utterly repugnant to God and subject to his wrath, 6-7

c. The conduct of Christians as light in the Lord must shine exposure and reproof on all immoral conduct, 8-14

2. A community whose controlling principle in all relations is "the will of the Lord," 5:15-6:9

(1) Must define and accept the principle, 5:15-21

a. Need for sharp discernment in an evil day, 15-17

b. Exhilaration to be found in the filling of the Spirit, 18-20

c. Must practice mutual subjection of ourselves to one another, 21

(2) Must apply the principle especially in the basic relations in the economy of the family household, 5:22-6:9

a. Relation of husband and wife, 5:22-33

(a) Wives subjecting themselves to husbands as to the Lord with the Church's relation to the Christ as their ideal, 22-24

(b) Husbands relating themselves to their wives in sentiment and conduct as the Christ to his Church, 25-31

(c) This high standard of the Christ and the Church is emphatically urged for Christian husbands and wives, 32-33

b. Relation of parents and children, 6:1-4

(a) Exhortation, ideal, and standard for children, 1-3

(b) Parents' (fathers') obligation to children, 4

c. Relations of masters and slaves, 5-9

(a) Slaves to interpret and discharge all duties as to the Lord who requites slave and freeman, 5-8

(b) Same principle applies to masters, plus the added responsibility of their position, 9a-b

(c) Both alike slaves of the Lord and subject to impartial judgment, 9c

VI. GLORIOUS WARFARE AND VICTORY OF THE CALLED—Chapter 6:10-20

1. Call to spiritual war, 10-18
   (1) Requires divine strength and full equipment, 10-11
   (2) Terrific nature of the conflict declared, 12
   (3) Items in the winning panopy, 13-17
   (4) Call for continuous, prayerful watchfulness, 18
2. God's Ambassador calls for special prayer for himself, 19-20
   (1) For the word when he speaks, 19a
   (2) For courageous freedom in revealing the "mystery of the gospel," 19b
   (3) For limitless courage when he must speak, 20

FINAL WORDS, 21-24

1. Information about himself, 21-22
2. Benediction on all genuine lovers of Jesus Christ, 23-24

Interpretation

Salutation 1:1-2

Paul identifies himself as an apostle of Christ Jesus, as having an authentic commission. He is a man "sent by Christ Jesus" and belonging to him. His commission is specific. It came to him by (through) a distinct act of God's will (θέλημα, not the general term θέλησις). Compare Paul's emphatic personal call as recorded by Luke in Acts 9 and as reported by himself in Acts 22:26. In the constraint, under the authority, and with the emphasis of that experience and conviction we find him at all times acting, speaking, planning, writing. Always he is God's ambassador in behalf of Christ with a sense that God is speaking through him (2 Cor. 5:18-20; Eph. 6:20).

He addresses "the saints"—people who have been dedicated, and have dedicated themselves, to God. They are such as are "in Christ Jesus" and in him are "faithful." Whether Paul is here addressing the particular group of saints in each church where the letter would be read is not wholly clear. The explanation of the fact that "in Ephesus" is not found in two of the oldest and most authentic manuscripts is highly plausible, namely: that the letter was to be read in all the churches in the province of Asia—and then elsewhere—and the local name could be inserted at each reading.

In any case, it is a message for all saints and will be meaningful in proportion as the saints are "also faithful." "Believing" and "faithful" are intimately interrelated. There is much discussion concerning which is meant here. The form of the word suggests the loyalty—faithfulness—of the saints. Yet we become "saints" by faith; and faithfulness is the active response toward Christ of those who have faith in Christ—in his person, his purpose, his work, his claim on us. Both terms are on the same Greek word stem, while the form found here seems to be used in both senses.

For all such saints the apostle bespeaks "grace" and "peace" from God in his capacity as our Father and from him who is our Lord, Jesus Christ. The grace and the peace, interrelated gifts, come from the Father God and equally from our Lord.

I

THE GLORIOUS PURPOSE AND PROJECTION—Chapter I

The purpose of world redemption, eternally in God and projected for accomplishment through the redeeming Son, is presented in a section which constitutes chapter 1.

1. It is given first in a condensed outline of the plan as it revolves successively around each of the persons in the Trinity (3-14). Then it is presented in the form of a prayer of gratitude for the saints already experiencing the call of grace, and of petition that they may be enabled to understand God's glorious purpose and the relation of the redeemed saints to the plan of God (15-21).

The three sections, introducing successively the Persons of the Trinity, all end in a phrase that emphasizes that every stage of the work of redemption and its outcome is to contribute to the glory of God in the expression of his grace and in its recognition (vv. 6, 12, 14). Nowhere in this Epistle or elsewhere in the New Testament is there any formal statement of the concept of the Trinity. Here, as elsewhere, there is distinct recognition of the Trinity and explicit use of the concept, and the use is such as involves necessarily the objective and active reality of the three Persons. Here, as always, where the Three appear, in purpose, function, and work they are entirely at one. The logical distinction is functional, but is so used as to require belief in its actuality. In no part of the Bible is God an abstract being. He is never the infinite Absolute of Philosophy. Always he is the immediately omnipresent Almighty Person manifesting himself in some characteristic activity.

Philosophically considered, all progress is by interaction of relatively distinct and counteracting forces or forms of activity which attain integration in unified results. In Christian philosophy, since all the process is divine, the different and relatively contrasting forms of action and procedure are each self-consistent by reason of being the expression of one divine Person. The conflicts and relative antagonisms are harmonized in the one end and one plan in which the three divine Persons unite. The Three constitute the One Godhead. But this analysis and harmonization of thought are not made in the Scriptures. It is assumed and its actuality affirmed without apology and without explanation, with only rare and general recognition that it constitutes a problem.

The Bible is not philosophy, nor is it theology. It is affirmation of Deity in action to achieve a purpose by a plan of working in history, as God deals with the materials at hand. Whenever the occasion seems to demand it, God's ultimate creation of the materials and situations is affirmed. Paul exemplifies this way of conceiving and declaring God in action. The infinite, eternal working God is thus Father, Son, Holy Spirit. Whatever aspect of the common concern of the Trinity falls to the primary concern of Father, Son, or Spirit, the Three are always One in interest and in outcome.

(1) The ultimate God whose worthiness is to be recognized in praiseful blessing is related to us and is approachable by us as "the God and Father of our Lord Jesus Christ." It is through him that we know God as fatherly and approach him in praise as our Father. It is he "who blessed us in every sort of blessing that is spiritual" in content and value. Such blessings are "in the realm of our heavenly relationships" and produce in us heavenly qualities. And all these blessings come from the Father to us "in Christ" who is God's sole channel of expressing himself graciously to men (3). This experience and this understanding of the experience corresponds exactly (καθώς) to the fact that God "chose us in Christ (ἐν αὐτῷ), before the foundation ("throwing-down") of the cosmic world (τοῦ κόσμου)."

His aim in the choice was "that we should be made holy and blameless in his sight." He desired to have as his own a group who were set apart for himself and whose dedication to his purpose would leave them with no lack, blameless (4). This choice was made "in a love that designated (marked off) us for experiencing complete sonship" (unto himself), and this was to be accomplished "through Jesus Christ." The only, sufficient ground for this choice and intention was the good pleasure of his own sovereign will (5). And the ultimate end of it all was "the praise of the glory of his grace," a praise which the universe would acclaim when it was seen how he had thus "bestowed his grace upon us in his goodness as expressed in his Beloved" (6).

(2) At this point the thought centers in the stewardship of history through the redeeming work of the Beloved Son, which in its turn issues in "the praise of his (God's) glory" (7-12). Through the Beloved Son, when we have come to be "in him, we have our redemption" as an experienced possession, procured for us and experienced by us "by means of his blood." This redemption includes "the removal of our trespasses." This great redemption is measured only by "the richness of God's grace" (7), which is so abundant that he "flooded us with it, as in all wisdom and understanding (8) he made known to us the inner purpose of his will." In all this he was acting "in accordance with the characteristic good will of his nature" (cf. v. 5, where this was affirmed of God's choice of us for redemption).

This gracious pleasure of God projected itself "in the Christ" (9) "with a view to such an administration of the complete cycle of the ages, as their opportunities unfold, as would cause all things to be headed up in the Christ." The all things here includes all "those in heaven" and all "those on earth," integrated in one harmonious whole (10).

It was in the carrying out of this gracious purpose of God "in Christ that we (Jews) were included, in God's plan," yes in the Christ "in whom we were even made (a part of) God's heritage, in the plan of him whose energy carries out all things in accordance with the counsel of his own will" (11; cf. 5, 9).

This claiming of "us who first among men and before his coming cherished hope in the Christ" had as its purpose that we should be a channel and means "unto the praise of his glory"

(12; cf. 6). The thought here is, not, as commonly understood, that the Jews were made God's heirs, whatever truth may be in that idea, but that God claimed the Jews for his peculiar heritage among men. This is the uniform use of the word in this Epistle, and it is in accord with the basic thought of the Old Testament with reference to Israel. It has been the calamity of the Jews and a gross error of Christians that they have reversed this order in fundamental thinking about the electing choice of God. The thought of the saved being heirs of God is a glorious concept found, e.g., in Romans 8:17; but it is not the usual form of the inheritance figure and is not so found in Ephesians.

(3) The part of the Holy Spirit in this glorious work of grace is also "unto the praise of God's glory" (13-14). Gentiles equally with Jews have their place in the Christ, even though neither they nor the Jews had known or recognized this fact previous to his coming. Turning to the Gentiles at this point, Paul says: "In whom, when you had heard the real content of the truth about the purpose of God's grace, as that interpretation came to you, the good news that his salvation was yours, and when you had put your faith in Christ, you, too, were stamped with the seal of God's ownership."

This seal came in the form of superhuman manifestations which attended each first reception of the gospel by a new racial group. It was first seen in the case of the Samaritan believers under Philip's ministry, and especially when Peter and John tested the genuineness of this experience by prayer and the laying on of hands (Acts 8:9-17).

It was repeated when Peter preached to Romans in the home of Cornelius and the Holy Spirit came upon them, convincing Peter and his associates that Romans were God's people through faith in Christ Jesus (Acts 10-11). As the early missionaries went with the gospel into new territory, their work was made effective "in the power," and was attested by "the demonstration of the Spirit" (1 Cor. 2:4).

In the Jerusalem Conference, Barnabas and Saul won the

approval of the entire body on their course in receiving various groups of Gentiles into full Christian fellowship by "rehearsing what signs and wonders God had wrought among the Gentiles through them" (Acts 15:12). The Holy Spirit had thus put the seal of salvation and God's claim of ownership upon each racial group as it was brought to accept the redemption of the Christ.

See also Acts 19:1-7, where Paul tested some disciples at Ephesus who had aroused his suspicion by asking whether they had received the Holy Spirit in connection with their baptism. Finding that they had no such seal on their profession, on further inquiry it developed that they did not know of the work of Jesus. Now they believed on him. Upon their being "baptized into the name of the Lord Jesus," "the Holy Spirit came upon them" so that "they spoke with tongues and prophesied." This was the seal of God's acceptance and ownership.

All these are examples of what Paul, here in Ephesians, means by saying that the Gentiles "were sealed with the Holy Spirit of promise." The Greek order is striking: "with the Spirit of the promise, the Holy" (13). In commissioning his disciples to make his gospel universal and all-comprehensive, Jesus had stressed "the promise of his Father" to send with them and upon them his Spirit, in whose power they were to achieve and without whose presence they were not even to begin.

In Ephesians 4:30 individual believers are said to have been "sealed unto the day of redemption" "in the Holy Spirit." The basic thought is the same there and in 1:13f. God has marked as his own what he claims and with which he is at work to complete his possession of it, by making it fit for its relation to him and his purpose. While the immediate reference to the sealing of the Holy Spirit is here to the miraculous manifestations of his presence and approval, that is by no means the exclusive reference. Any attestation of our salvation by the Spirit is such a seal and pledge of ultimate complete redemption. The reference in 4:30 is presumably to inner experience. This is clearly true of Romans 8:16-17, 29, where the feature of assurance is central. The seal idea is not employed in these two passages, but "the firstfruits of the Spirit" are the assurance of the full outcome, and the inner testimony of conviction supported by the witness of the Spirit is assurance of sonship. In 2 Corinthians 1:20-21, God seals us in Christ and gives us his "Yea" and "Amen" as "the earnest of the Spirit in our hearts."

Thus we are not to think of "the sealing," which is the "pledge" of all that is to be accomplished in us by God's grace, as something apart from and in addition to the experience of redemption. Rather it is the beginning of that good work in us, which, being God's work, he "will perfect unto the day of Jesus Christ" (Phil. 1:6). It is the "firstfruits" of the full harvest to follow that constitutes the seal, as in Romans 8:23.

The phrase in Ephesians 1:14 that presents the thought means "that with which he is working." All translations which make the statement to mean a guarantee that we are assured of complete possession of an inheritance do violence to the motif and movement of the entire passage as well as to the syntax of the particular statement. (See especially the surprising rendering in RSV). Thus in the sealing the Holy Spirit is the specific evidence of our being God's inheritance until the redemption of that which he claims and is working with (τõυ περιποιημένου) is complete. When God's inheritance is thus fully possessed by him, perfected by his gracious working, we shall be "for (unto) the praise of his glory" (14).

It is to be especially noted that Paul begins this section by addressing the Gentiles (13) and telling of their being sealed for God, but that when he comes to explain (14) that the sealing is the pledge of complete possession of the completely redeemed, he switches to the first person "pledge of the inheritance (by God) of us." Here the "us" is all the redeemed, Jews, who are the "we" of verse 12, and Gentiles, who are the "ye" of verse 13. This is in accordance with one of Paul's central emphases: that the redeemed of all races are all one in Christ Jesus (Gal. 3:28, etc.). This emphasis is elaborated in the second chapter.

2. Having outlined the divine purpose and plan, in which each

of the Persons of the Trinity shares, and having stressed that the glory of the grace of God is to be accomplished in this work of redemption and blessing, Paul further develops the thought in a prayer that the redeemed may understand God's intention in calling them (15-21). It is to be insisted that it is God's hope and God's heritage which Paul has in mind here as his ground of appeal and assurance. Almost unanimously the expositors and the translators have failed to see and hold to the apostle's center of gravity here. Man, redeemed man, is very generally made the center. Thought is centered on man's blessing, man's hope, man's glory in the redemptive work. Important and blessed as this is for us, upon examination and reflection this is clearly not Paul's approach here.

Elsewhere he does direct thought concerning the glory of our salvation to its meaning for the saved. We are the heirs of God, jointly with Jesus Christ, (Rom. 8:12-25; 2 Cor. 6:18; Gal. 3:29, 4:7, etc.; and cf. 1 John 3:1; Rev. 21:7, etc.). In Ephesians the interest of God and his glory in redemption are steadily held as the starting point, the focus, and the end of the entire argument. Paul is consistent in the development of his discussion; and we should follow consistently in our interpretation and application of what he here presents.

(1) The prayer begins in praise to God for "the called." His praise and his petition grow naturally and inevitably out of his contemplation and exposition of the infinite unity and glory of God's work of redemption, and specifically out of his joy in seeing that Gentiles are experiencing the assurance of their being included in God's heritage. He thinks of himself as caught up into participation in this glorious work. "On this account I, too, having heard of the faith in the Lord Jesus found in different groups of you Gentiles, the faith which characterizes all the saints, do not cease giving thanks over you."

In Colossians 1:3-12 we have a general parallel to Ephesians 1:15-19 and 3:14-19. There are more or less exact parallels at several points. Thus Colossians 1:4 has been drawn upon to solve a difficult reading in the best manuscripts at 1:15. The words, *"and the love,"* are lacking, but are supplied in many texts and have been accepted in most translations. It is a delicate and difficult question in textual criticism. If the words were not used here by Paul, we have a problem in grammatical construction. "The faith among you in the Lord Jesus and unto all the saints," omitting "and the love," is very unusual and difficult to define with any certainty. Also "the faith among you," or, in the Greek order, "the among you faith," while not wholly exceptional, is a rare form of statement and not easy to grasp. It is, to put in English the Greek idiom, not "your faith," which of course we have many times, but "the along your faith," or "down-at-you" (κατὰ, ὑμᾶς).

The preposition (κατὰ) is used idiomatically in a distributive sense. To the various suggestions offered to solve the difficulty, one is added that may resolve both the unusual construction and the apparent omission of "the love." Paul is thinking not of one group of Gentile believers in one location only, but of the Gentiles as a whole as included in God's redemption through the Christ. The Greek idiom, "down along" (κατὰ plus an accusative case), or group by group, would serve his thought of generalizing faith as found among Gentiles. "The faith in the Lord Jesus which is found with you, and you, and you—group after group—and which obtains in all the saints, as the common experience of those who are in Christ." This would meet the grammatical difficulties and would fit perfectly Paul's teaching elsewhere, particularly in 3:6-8 of this Epistle.

Still, it would be a severe condensation of thought, and after all the easier way may be correct, to suppose that "and the love" dropped out by the oversight of some copyist and his error was repeated by the majority of copyists who followed him. "The love which ye have toward all the saints," as in Colossians, is certainly a fitting and a highly important aspect of Christian experience.

There should be no difficulty over Paul's "having heard of the faith" of Ephesians or any other Gentiles. Of course he was hearing of this all along as well as witnessing it wherever he went. The aorists of participles and verbs here are gnomic, of customary experience. It is not the time connection that is in mind, except remotely, but the logical relation of impulsive and rational response. Whenever the faith of Gentiles (or Jews, for that matter) came to his attention, he began giving thanks to his God. In fact, the reminders were constant, and he can say, "I do not cease giving thanks over you, and making specific mention of you upon all occasions of my praying" (16). It was his normal reaction and his fixed habit. He was always Christ's apostle to the Gentiles, and he held their converts always in his heart. He never "left off" praying thankfully about them.

(2) He defines the nature and scope of his prayer for these saints (17-21).

a. His first petition is that God "would give to you the Spirit who gives comprehensive insight and revelation in the sphere of the accurate understanding of him." He wishes them (all of us) to know God in his saving purpose and activity, in his nature and in his work in history. For this only the Spirit of God is adequate. He must bring to us the wisdom to see and to grasp, and he must then reveal to us and enable us to reveal to others, "the mystery of the gospel."

In the atmosphere of the glory of redemption in which Paul moves, he addresses his petition to "the God of our Lord Jesus Christ." God is, of course, as so often expressed, the Father of Jesus. Just why that is omitted here we may not be sure. We come to God through Jesus Christ in order that he may become our Father. As enabling us to come thus to God, Jesus is serving God and is functionally subordinate to him. This form of statement may identify Jesus with his saints in achieving the glory of God. It is in harmony with the emphasis throughout this section of the Epistle.

In this relation, and seeing the transcendent glory which the redemptive work is to bring to God, he is also to be thought of as "the Father of glory." This may be understood as the all-glorious Father; or, perhaps better, the source of all true glory; or he to whom all glory is due and to be given. Through his Spirit in Christ Jesus he will give to his saints the capacity to make him glorious in history and in the consummation when as "the Lord of glory . . . (the Christ) shall come to be glorified in his saints" (2 Thess. 1:9-10); and when "every tongue shall confess that Jesus Christ is Lord, to the glory of God the Father" (Phil. 2:11). Because Paul is dealing with this process that is to culminate in the complete glorification of God as Father, of all, he makes his prayer for "his saints" "to the Father of Glory" (cf. 1 Cor. 15:24-28).

b. His petition is that with open-hearted clarity the saints may know our significance to God (18-21). In preparation for this great and greatly important knowledge, "the eyes of the heart must be opened." That is sound psychology and epistemology. Right attitude of soul is the first condition of all knowing. The fear of the Lord is truly the beginning of knowledge and of wisdom (Prov. 1:7; 9:10). True in all learning and all understanding, it is emphatically true in the understanding of God and his salvation. Here pre-eminently "the secret of the Lord is with them that fear him" (Psalm 25:14). As declared here, and emphasized in chapter 3, the knowledge of God's way of redemption requires revelation. The Spirit opens the eyes of the heart and of the mind. In Luke 24 we read how Jesus opened the minds of the disciples in the upper room that they might understand the Scriptures in relation to his resurrection and his kingdom program.

Paul affirms this item in what appears to be an accusative absolute. He uses the perfect participle, "the eyes of your heart having been opened," emphasizing this as a definite attitude of soul essential for grasping the great realities involved. With this preparation the Spirit will enable us to know the several aspects of the Christian movement, its scope, its methods, its designed outcome. The word for know is that of clear discernment (ἰδ-). It is not research or reasoning, however much these may be employed in the process; it is basic knowledge which has the quality of intuition.

What, then, does Paul so earnestly desire the saints to know? There are three items, clearly articulated by introducing each with the interrogative what? (τίς . . . τί).

(a) First is, "That ye may know what is the hope of your calling" (18a). As already pointed out, this is to be understood of God's hope in calling us, not what we may hope in that he has called us. This Epistle is the outline of God's purpose and objective in Christ and his Church. That this is the right understanding here will be confirmed as we proceed. God's calling of no man reaches its final goal in the man. He is called to a place and part in the vast enterprise of God with humanity. Each Christian needs to know what God's hope is for Christianity as a whole; and what each needs to find is the use God intends to make of him in fulfilling that hope.

It may be objected that God cannot hope, since he knows. But that would be to interpose metaphysics to check religious insight and consecration. The Bible is intensely practical. The absolute God must make himself relative with reference to men. So the Bible speaks of God in terms of practical understanding. Only thus do we know God. He must deal with us on the finite plane and in terms of finite personality. When we seek ultimate understanding and security, we reflect that God has condescended to act on our level but is still infinitely beyond us.

(b) "That ye may know . . . what is the wealth of the glory of his inheritance in his saints" (18b). Here it would seem almost impossible to escape the true idea of Paul: the wealth which God sees and will realize by being glorified in his saints. But for our persistent tendency to think of what we get in Christ, no one would ever think of God's wealth of glory "in his saints" as meaning "for his saints." Salmond (Exp. Gr. Test.) sees the force of this but even then adopts the erroneous interpretation. Goodspeed and Moffatt evade in ambiguous phrases, Weymouth seems to accept the true meaning. RSV misses the point as to the hope but accepts it as to the wealth of glory. The thought of God's inheritance in his people is so frequent in the Old Testament as to make citation needless. Exodus 34:9, Psalm 28:9, and Deuteronomy 9:29 may be taken as examples. These examples will answer any possible misgiving on the ground that God does not inherit his saints from any source outside himself. That is one of the constant concepts of the Old Testament as applied to Israel.

(c) The third item of this knowledge calls for more elaboration. It has to do with God's resources for possessing his inheritance and so realizing his hope in his redeemed people. The hope, the inheritance, the power are all God's, and the glory is all his. Yet man is the object of it all. The glory of God is in gaining the complete, free response of man with power joyously to accept the will of God in filial love and full co-operation. Thus God works in man and enlists man in co-operative response to work through to completion his own salvation, which will consist in man individually and corporately willing and doing that which is well-pleasing unto God. Ephesians is the elaboration of this great ideal which Paul states in pregnant exhortation in Philippians 2:12-13.

More fully in Philippians 1:8-11 Paul has a close parallel to his prayer here in our passage. "God is my witness, how I yearn over all (of) you (having been made to share) in the compassionate concern of Christ Jesus. And I am praying for this: that your love ever more and more, with clear understanding and unfailing (every) discernment, will overflow into your discriminating (among) things that differ, (and) that (thus) you may be transparently blameless—(literally, without flaw when tested in sunlight)—(as you come) into the (perfect) day of Christ. This will result from your having come into full fruitbearing of righteousness, (that productiveness which comes in us) through Jesus Christ—(cf. the Vine and the branches of John 15)—(which abounds) unto the glory and praise of God" (cf. 1 Thess. 1:3).

In so great an enterprise, with so glorious an end, in which God's hope is fulfilled in his inheritance, the divine energy of God is the only power for producing the outcome and working in all stages of the process. We need to know "what is the superabundant greatness of his dynamic (which he releases) into us who believe." In order to stress the limitlessness of God's power for his purpose, and also to relate believers to the unity of God's activity in redemption, Paul now affirms that his dynamic in believers is "on the scale of the active energy of the gripping strength of his might (19) which he put forth in the Christ when he raised him from among the dead" (20a).

With God, rescuing lost men from their spiritual death, raising Christ Jesus from his physical death and from his spiritual defeat by sin in men, and the perfecting of the redemption of men through their faith in Jesus Christ are all aspects of one undertaking. So the power by which the work of full salvation proceeds is the same power that raised the Christ from death and from sin's temporary and superficial defeat of love in that death. Here we read that "the Christ"—not "Jesus"—was raised, because it was not as one human being that Jesus died and was raised, but as God's anointed Servant-Son, for the undertaking of redeeming humanity. Not to succeed in the enterprise of Christianity would be to have failed in Christ, which would negate God; and that is gloriously unthinkable.

In this passage (19-20a) Paul has exhausted the vocabulary of the Greek language to set forth God's power for achieving his goal. Seven different terms indicating power in various aspects are employed to enable us to see the Eternal God working at his masterpiece. Here in the midst of verse 20, Paul extends his definition of God's work in Christ and prepares for a new stage in his outline of God's plan for effective control of human history and destiny. Not only did God raise Jesus Christ from death, he "seated him at his own right hand in the realms and relations of heaven" (20b-21a). There the Christ is, exalted clear above (ὑπεράνω) every form or order and rule in the universe; and his position is permanent—permanent because it is due to the essential nature of the relation between him and his Father on the one hand and between him and the world order on the other hand.

We may compare for basic ideas here Psalm 8, where man is placed just under God and crowned lord of all the works of God's hands; and Hebrews 2:5ff., where the psalm is quoted and the comment added that "we see not yet all things subjected to man. But him who for a little time was made somewhat less than (in comparison with) angels we do look upon, Jesus, through the experience of death crowned with glory and honor." Then in 1 Corinthians 15:27-28, in line with verse 20, we find in another setting all the features of the resurrection power and honor of the Christ achieving the absolute supremacy of God in the universe.

We are, then, on safe ground in understanding that in the sentence before us there is more than the exaltation of the crucified and risen Christ. He is put at the administrative and constructive head of the growing order of the universe. Not in honor only or primarily, but in functional position and authority he is "up over," at the head of, "every form of government, and authority and power and dominion, and every title of sovereignty, not only (as these obtain) in this age but also in the ensuing (age)" (21). We must understand the all as distributive here, "every," not general, "all."

This list of forms of orderly administration we do not think of as listing such orders in any scientifically accurate or exhaustive way. It is a general, theoretical arrangement in which the purpose is to affirm the complete and exclusive headship of the exalted Christ over the entire system of world-order, whatever it is. The affirmation is positive and direct, not polemical or contrasted with any erroneous theories of fictitious systems.

In 3:10 and Colossians 1:16 some actual organization of rule and authority is recognized. In the latter passage, in its setting in the paragraph 13-17, this headship of an orderly universe is comprehensively affirmed, while a "dominion of darkness" is also recognized, from which we are "rescued and transferred to the kingdom of the Son of God's love." This Son "is the exact concretion of the invisible God, born prior to the whole process; in whom all that is, in heaven and earth, seen and unseen, were created, be they thrones or lordships, dominions or sovereignties; they were all created through him and for his use; he is before them all and in him they all stand integrated." In

Romans 8:38, 1 Peter 3:22, systematized powers are recognized with the suggestion that they may be antagonistic to the order of redemption and righteousness. In Colossians 2:13-19 the antagonizing orders of power and systems of religion are definitely recognized, as indeed they are in one form or another in many scriptures. We shall meet them further in Ephesians.

3. The glorious purpose of God is now shown to be effected in and by the relation of Christ and the Church (22-23).

(1) With purpose and in plan God is declared to have "arranged all things in orderly system under the feet" of the reigning Christ (22a). As yet this is ideal and potential in a disordered, rebellious, and morally and socially chaotic world. Here is a task. The Christ is not only Lord but Redeemer. And, so far as our race is concerned, he must redeem in order to rule. God is calling out a people for his own possession and service in achieving his rule of redemption and righteousness in our earth. The Christ, with the blood of his cross and with the power of his resurrection, and now with the authority of his universal lordship, is from this point considered in his incarnation and in his incorporation in humanity. The people of God, the saints of the Saviour, have been gathered and sealed in the first section of the chapter. In the second section the apostle has prayed that they may know what it all means, for God and for his exalted, sovereign Son. Now they must see and accept the relation that subsists between them and the Christ. They must see what it must mean for them of responsible privilege.

(2) Here the redeemed people of God in Christ are named in their organic relations. They are God's Church. To them as the Church, God gave this universal Ruler for its Head. He is God's supreme, sole representative in the order of the universe. He is given to the Church to be its Head over all things. He is established above and over all things. Now as its Head he brings this universal overlordship to the Church to which he has been given by God. The Church is thus to share in his command and control of all that is, working with him as he works in them for the ends in view.

The Church must here be understood in its universal, all-comprehensive, spiritual sense. The relation between the Christ and his Church is organic in the spiritual sense. This is expressed by saying "the Church which is his Body." Head and body constitute one organism. Each is incomplete without the other. The Christ is Redeemer, actually, only when and in the measure that there are redeemed people. They are redeemed by him. In each case he incorporates the redeemed in himself and into his redeeming expression and activity. This is more than a figure of speech. It is a reality both mystically and actually. We become part not only of the body of his redeemed, but parts of his redeeming Body. He extends his work and his results through the members of his Body.

This is why he gave his commission to his first believers and gives it to all believers. And this is why he so strongly enjoins upon us all that "apart from him we can do nothing," "can produce no fruit"; and why he promises that his Spirit will come upon all his members and vitalize them both with his life and with his characteristic activity in redemption. The Church is, first of all, organic, not an organization or an institution. It is a living organism. This is especially amplified in chapter 4.

The members of the Church are also organized in churches. The organization should always be subordinate to function and serve the function. In Ephesians, as in Colossians, the Church is not discussed except as the living expression of the Christ. It is not strictly proper to speak of the Church in the sense of Christ's Body as "invisible." It is invisible in the sense that union with him is not physical and hence there are no physical tests of our union with him. Nor does organizational union with a church prove membership in Christ and therefore in his spiritual Body.

Yet Christians are known by their fruits, by their standards, their ideals, their behaviour, their aims and efforts and achievements in living. The organized church confirms those who are committed to the experience and the mission of the Church as organic with the Christ. All this is so important that it has been discussed more fully in a special section of this work. Here we seek to follow Paul in his concept of the Church as spiritually and functionally, ethically and actively organic with the Christ. It is produced by his grace, and he is completing himself in his Body. Head and Body are one (22b).

(3) At this point Paul takes us further into this intimate interdependence of Christ and Church (23), and prepares the way for further analysis of the relation in succeeding chapters. The Church is "the fullness of him who is coming into the fulfilment of (as to) all things in all respects. "All things" is emphatic, "the all things" (τὰ πάντα), as repeatedly in this connection.

Whether the participle "fulfilling" is passive or middle, or as middle essentially active has been much discussed. The question does not seem vitally important. The thought is clear enough if we are able to grasp it. God's purpose in history is fulfilling, being fulfilled. The Christ is the active Deity in fulfilling. Yet as the functional redeeming Deity, he is being fulfilled as his work proceeds. All that God does in history, and in this Epistle in cosmic process as well, he does by and through the Christ. Hence the Christ is being fulfilled while he is also fulfilling the purpose of God and bringing God's glory into its fulness. We may approach the fulfilling from each of these three standpoints.

The new item which Paul adds here concerns the Church. The Christ is assumed as the full manifestation, expression, redeeming agent of God. What Paul now wishes us to see is that the Church is the full expression of the Christ. All that he achieves in personal redemption goes *de facto* into the Church. Our difficulty lies chiefly in the fact that the organized Church, as seen in the churches, so inadequately expresses the Christ. He cannot be this, not just this. Nor can we wholly escape the difficulty by any recourse to the "invisible" Church, or the concept of the Church as constituted of the actually redeemed. For all its members are both redeemed as a fact and are in process of redemption, with imperfections, limitations, sins in us all, to be overcome and eliminated in the continued work of God's grace in Christ Jesus. The ideally perfect Church is always empirically imperfect in the churches.

Yet here is the concept, the ideal, the call, the promise which we may—must—accept, and commit ourselves to its actualization. Christ in the world is what his Church is. His Church is challenged to be what he is. Head and Body are one entity as the spiritual factor in God's human economy. This union of Christ and the Church for the glory of God is the climax of the first stage of Paul's exposition of the meaning of Christianity as the controlling factor in history.

II

THE GLORIOUS EXPERIENCE OF THE CALLED—Chapter 2

Having outlined the Christian Calling in its divine projection, having prayed that the Called shall know and accept their significance in God's plan and work in creating the Calling, and having linked the Christ and the Church of the Called in one unit of reality and function in history, the apostle now comes to consider the Christian Calling from the standpoint of its human experience. The connection is very close with the exposition in chapter 1. The thought has not moved in the realm of abstraction, nor of mere theory. At every point the living, active God is very present to consciousness. The Christ and the Spirit are seen and felt at their work in producing saints by redemption and sealing, and incorporating them in one Body of the progressively completing Christ as the Head of the Church Body. Now the argument leads to looking in while the work goes on in detail.

1. And first, the individual experience of the calling of God's saving grace. Here we see the new man being created by Christ Jesus (1-10).

The paragraph starts off "And you," accusative case, but pauses to describe the condition of "you"—all of us—and resumes the sentence in a slightly new form at verse 4. Thus we begin with a graphic description of

(1) The dead material with which God must work (1-3). Starting off with "you" Gentiles whom he had spoken of in 1:14 and 15f., we see Paul's mind reaching out to comprehend all the redeemed as having been participants in the depraved human nature and conduct, by reason of which all men are ethically and

spiritually dead. God must begin his glorious work of redemption always with this sort of dead material.

Paul has here in mind comparison of man in moral deadness with the physically dead Christ (1:20) whom God raised. By the same power and with the same ultimate purpose he raised dead souls. Their spiritual death, actual and hopeless but for God's gracious vitalizing, is emphasized here with elaboration. Paul calls them, metaphoricaly, "dead bodies." Their death was by means of (instrumental case) their transgressions ("falls" παραπτώμασι) and also by reason of their sinful tendencies. We might expect here *sins* in the sense of sinful acts, corresponding with "falls." This would be normally ἁμαρτήμασι; but the word is ἁμαρτίαις. This seems to be by deliberate choice to say by *principles of sinfulness,* rather than saying by sinful acts. Paul is going to the roots of our failure.

In verse 2 their sins are presented as the sphere of activity in which these redeemed at one time lived and acted: "in which transgressions and sins you formerly were in the habit of living ('walked-about') in accordance with (the standards of) the course of this world order"—literally "the age," in the sense of the spirit of the age. The spirit of the age is further defined as being controlled by, and so "corresponding to the ruler of the authority of the air." The moral atmosphere of the world is under the control of the ruler of the realm of evil, and so the moral atmosphere of human living is corrupted by "the spirit who now exercises rule among the sons of disobedience." "Now" contrasts with "formerly," and has the sense of "still." The redeemed were at that time part of this evil order. They have been rescued from it but it still goes on and all who accept it are so normally, persistently and unanimously given to disobedience to God and his standards as properly to be described as "children of the principle of disobedience."

Paul is not yet done with this dark subject of spiritual death. In verse 3 he universalizes it and goes yet more deeply into its nature and source, reminding us of his intense and intensive treatment in Romans. "Among these" children of disobedience "we all (changing to first person) formerly conducted-our-lives," when we acted "in the" realm of control by the "appetites of our natural man." "Flesh" is regularly used by Paul in the sense of unregenerate human nature. In the terms of certain modern ethical systems, Paul would say "when we followed our natural impulses and urges." We were then "doing regularly the things willed by the flesh and by the (uninhibited) ideas of the mind"; i.e., whatever we took a notion to do. In this stage and state "we were by (our very) nature the offspring of wrath, even as the rest (still and always) are." Being born into sin and for self-willed disobedience, "against which the wrath of God is revealed from heaven" (Rom. 1:18f.), men may be said to be naturally "children of wrath." Such, then, is the human material with which God begins his glorious work.

(2) With verse 4 Paul resumes his statement, begun at verse 1 and immediately broken off, of the life-giving experience of God's grace through faith (4-6).

Notwithstanding, indeed just because of, the utterly hopeless condition of natural man, "God himself ('the God') being rich in mercy, because of the great (literally 'much') love with which he loved us even while we were dead by reason of our trespasses, brought us to life along with the Christ." He loved us while we were in death. Most translators construe "while we were dead" with "made us alive." This involves a sort of tautology. The marvel is that he so loved us in our repulsive death that he gave his Son to die for us, in order that he might make us alive.

At this point Paul breaks in with an emphatic, ejaculatory affirmation. He cannot wait to say it at its logical place, where indeed he will repeat it. Right into the midst of a series of three co-ordinate verbs defining God's saving action he throws the declaration. "It is by grace that you are in the saved state!" The order of words and the perfect tense require this rendering.

In dealing with Jesus Christ who died in behalf of us dead sinners, God linked us up with the dead Saviour. Hence (a) "he made us alive along with him"; (b) "he raised us up from death along with him"; (c) "he set us down along with him in the heavenly realms and relations." All this he did for us and in us because he dealt with us "in Christ Jesus." In his own thinking of us through the Christ who became incarnate and sacrificed himself in our behalf, God incorporated us in Christ Jesus. When he died Christ Jesus was sacrificially dead with us for whom he had died by the will of his Father. When God raised him from the dead, in intention, in corporate activity, in anticipation of objective actual experience, he raised us up also, having thought of giving us life as he made him alive and by anticipation extending the vitalizing energy into us.

And inasmuch as the regenerate are to be united with the Christ in his Church Body, God ideally and prospectively lifted us up along with the Christ in his exaltation. To be sure, Paul stops short of saying that he seated us at his own right hand along with the Christ. That is a right exclusive for the divine personal Son and Lord. Such clearly seems to be the form of the apostle's thought, and it fits into the movement of the whole Epistle, and is consonant with the character and attitude of God in the gospel of redemption.

We do not need, therefore, to think of this as being a proleptic declaration of literal bodily resurrection of the saints. Paul had definitely repudiated that idea already in 1 Corinthians 15. Least of all, do we find here some vague reference to sharing rule with Christ in the final consummation. Paul is thinking of that spiritual and moral regeneration wherein we "do reckon ourselves to be dead indeed unto sin, but alive unto God in Christ Jesus." (See Rom. 6:11 and the whole paragraph 1-11.) Our right and our capacity so to reckon ourselves lie in the fact that God has so reckoned concerning us and imparts to us through our faith in Jesus Christ his own life to be our new life. (Compare Col. 2:12-13 and 3:1-4.) In thus reckoning, humbly and meekly but still boldly, we find ourselves in harmony with God's own reckoning. Faithful is the saying: "If we died with him, we shall also live with him: if we patiently endure, we shall also reign with him" (2 Tim. 2:11f.). We are not to be troubled about the time factors in all this. God's acts are not, strictly speaking, time conditioned. The sequence here is of logic and life, not of time and finite causation.

(3) One aspect of God's saving grace through Jesus Christ

is the demonstration which it gives to the universe of his nature (7). All this is done, for one reason: "in order thereby to demonstrate (to show-in-the-fact) in the ages as they come along the surpassing wealth of his grace (which is of the essence of his nature) in that he was gracious toward us in Christ Jesus." "His graciousness upon us" is a revelation and demonstration of the quality of God's nature which causes him to do for his creatures according to their needs and not according to what they deserve. In our case he has laid hold on dead sinners and exalted them to sharing the work and the glory of his Son Jesus Christ. In this his grace is indeed "going beyond": it is infinite. We see this idea of demonstrating his character again at 3:10f.

(4) God's wisdom and grace are further seen in his pre-provision for the life activity of those whom he re-creates (8-10). It all redounds to the glorification of God "because" it is only "by grace" that "you have been saved, through faith." And that experience was none of your doing, "and that not out from you." You did not go out seeking God and his grace. He originated it—and effected it—"God's gift" (8). And it was not wrought out by any merit or labor of yours. It is not "out of works, so that no one at all may boast" (9). "For we are definitely a product of his, having been created in Christ Jesus" as something new. We are fitted in our spiritual creation for good works and so are set to do them (ἐπὶ). But they are not works that in any sense procure our salvation but unfailingly flow from our salvation and give it body and reality. They are works "which he made ready beforehand in order that in them we should have our sphere of activity" (10).

2. The new humanity created "by the blood of the cross" occupies our attention in the latter half of chapter 2 (11-22). We are re-created as individuals, but we are not as such left in isolation. The experience has its meaning in social relations and in social solidarity. We must never forget from what we have been saved, nor the means by which we are saved. And we must go on to see and accomplish the social meaning of our salvation and of our relation to God, who is out in Christ to reconcile the world unto himself. Paul still keeps in mind his immediate purpose of

interpreting for Gentile Christians their meaning in the purpose of God for humanity. Yet he sets the particular interest in the context of God's cosmic program and grounds his teachings in principles that apply to and transcend all racial, social, or other sectional distinctions. He universalizes each particular problem and principle.

In developing his conception of the new social group which God is producing by his regeneration of human individuals, the apostle employs a number of analogies. In the paragraph immediately before us the Church is not named, nor is its predicate appositive, the Body of the Christ. That is for him much more than an analogy: it is a mystical, existential reality. He has made that emphatic at the end of chapter 1. He will return to it in chapters 3 and 4. Here he employs analogies, which are also much more than mere illustrations. The redeemed as a related group constitute a new commonwealth with equality in citizenship. They are the household of God. Coming out of various racial and other groupings, they are being combined in one unitary architectural unit. Yes, they are being built into a sacred temple for God's spiritual occupancy. Most significant of all in this paragraph, the redeemed constitute a new type of humanity, united in peaceful and harmonious fellowship. We must look at the argument in detail.

(1) Keep always in mind the contrast between the "then" and the "now" (11-13).

The place of the Jews and their historic position in relation to God and to his plans was far more prominent in the first century Christian consciousness than it was subsequently. Incidentally, this would argue against dating this Epistle in the second century. Beginning as a movement within Judaism and employing the religious concepts and terminology of the Hebrew religion, especially of the moral law, the prophetic ideology and the liturgy of the Psalms, Christian thinking largely assumed the standpoint of the priority and basic truth of the Jewish religion. And we must continue to think of the continuity or "the Hebrew-Christian" religion, even when, as we must, we transcend and leave behind all claim or thought of priority or superiority of any group within the grace of God. In principle Abraham was the first Christian. Paul rightly claimed to preach the same "word of faith" which Moses taught (Rom. 10:6-10); and he elaborately develops the truth that God's promise to Abraham that he should be the "father of many nations" has, by divine intention, fulfilment in the incorporation of many nations in the divine family through faith (Rom. 4). All the Epistle to Galatians is development of the thesis that "they that are of faith, the same are sons of Abraham" (3:7). The plan of God and the people of God are one through all history, when rightly understood and accepted.

"Wherefore," referring to the preceding paragraph as a whole, Gentile Christians are urged to "keep-in-mind" their former utterly hopeless condition, a hopelessness in which "we all" shared, whatever claims we may have thought we had to the favor of God. The linear present asks us not just to recall but to keep in our minds what the marvel of God's grace has done for us.

"At that time and condition" (καιρὸς is more than a time designation), before your hearing and believing your salvation from God (1:13), "you, the nations in (the classification which the Jews and the Jewish Scriptures throughout make on the basis of the) flesh." . . . Here Paul breaks off for further explication, to return to his sentence at verse 12 with a fresh beginning of his object clause that states what he wishes us to remember.

The words qualifying and amplifying the "you" are not integrated into a complete sentence. They lose force if we try to construct a full sentence, or sentences, of them. They turn off into ejaculations, which lose an element of sarcasm and scorn of the superficial distinction unless translated as ejaculatory. "You" are "those who are called 'uncircumcision' by that which calls itself 'circumcision'; in the flesh! made-by-hand!" The distinction, he is saying, is both superficial, "in the flesh" only; and artificial, "handmade." It has no basis in nature and cannot be the basis for any essential religious distinction. Paul would—and does—take this position with reference to all ceremonial acts, "sacraments." They may have their value. Rightly understood, they do have value. But always they are potentially delusive.

They should never be made a ground of pride or contempt or of divisive distinction among regenerate, believing, redeemed people.

Now (12) the clause begins afresh: "keep-in-mind . . . that you were at that stage (probably the best word for the Greek καιρὸς, time, or season, usually) without a Christ." Usually "Christ," markedly in this Epistle, is the title and has the article, if it stands alone, without "Jesus," or "Lord," or both. Wherever the article is lacking, we need to look for the reason and seek the special shade of thought. In this case Gentiles are not merely outside "the Christ" of Hebrew promise and Jewish hope. They had no Christ expectation at all. Not only were they, as Paul now adds, "aliens," with no rights or hopes, "from" the standpoint of "the covenants of the promise."

"The promise," which became the only line of messianic hope and of divine promise, was that embodied in covenants, such as that with Abraham and the other patriarchs; renewed with the congregation of Israel at its various stages; and specifically reaffirmed with the holy Remnant of the faithful in the prophets; especially brought to climax with the pledges made to the Servant of Jehovah. It was historically a covenant with the descendants of Abraham and fulfilled in Jesus of Nazareth, the Christ, the Saviour. Having no share, by claim or concession, in that line, the Gentile peoples were peoples "without a hope"—literally, in emphatic construction, "a hope not having." It is not strange that the manuscripts differ as to this reading.

Further, and to reach the tragic climax, the Gentiles were "(ἄθεοι) God-less in the world order (ἐν τῷ κόσμῳ)." They had failed to find the true God in all the order of nature and history, since he is known only when seen in the Christ. Paul does not, of course, mean to deny all knowledge of God to men outside the Hebrew revelation (Cf. Rom. 1:18-23). He does not mean to say that the heathen are "atheists" in our modern sense of rejecting and denying God. It is men who do not have God as he is, and must be, known for salvation. (See 1 Cor. 8:5-6.) Such, then, is the hopeless plight of the nations before God came to them in the power of the gospel of Jesus Christ.

See now the contrast which the apostle stresses (13). "Now"

is in strong adversion to "then" (11) and "at that stage" (12). By its position and by its being in the locative case of the adverb (νυνὶ δε) and by use of the adversive conjunction, literally "in the now," the idea is made as emphatic as possible. The new condition is theirs because they are "in Christ Jesus," "through whom you who then were in the condition of being a long way off have come to be near (to God) in the blood of the Christ." He is now your Christ and the relation is complete—a blood relation—his life having become your life. (Cf. Col. 1:18-23; 3:1-4.) For the condition of being near to God or far from him, we may compare especially Isaiah 57:19; and the contrast is often found in Psalms. Isaiah does not use it to contrast Jews and Gentiles but makes the distinction on the basis of ethical and spiritual condition. Paul had come to adopt the same position in all its fulness. He leaves no people as such far from God on ethnic grounds, and makes none nigh unto him on any basis except "in Christ Jesus."

(2) Without so much as breaking his sentence, Paul now passes on to unfold the fact that God's peace is for all men through the Christ. And peace with God means that among men all divisive distinctions and all antagonistic feelings are abolished. Only thus is peace established (14-16). They who were, naturally, formerly at a distance have come to be near in the Christ "because it is he who is our peace." Here Paul swings into the first person, for he is thinking now in the realm of the common Christian experience. The Christ has become "our peace" "by making both the two (literally 'the both') one and by destroying the wall, namely, enmity, that broke up into fragments (what in God's ideal was one)." The Greek and the English idioms are so unlike here as to make verbal translation impossible. Verbally the Greek would go in English words, "having loosed the middle-wall of the fragment, the enmity." The thought is clear. Racial and religious enmity had broken into fragments what ideally and in the intention of God is one humanity. This vicious principle, by its customs, conventions, and teachings had erected a wall that kept the races apart from each other. Not one but many such walls exist. Paul was in this connection thinking

of that which separated Jews and Gentiles as a whole.

This wall—and we must include all separating walls—the Christ abolished "in his flesh." The exact bearing of "in his flesh" is doubtful, although the general idea is not difficult. It means that in his incarnation humanity (flesh) he dissolved the separating wall of enmity. The enmity was strengthened and even sanctified from the Jewish side, at least, and often from the side of the heathen religions, by "the law of the commandments" embodied and made imperative by being formulated "in dogmas." This formal law the Christ "rendered inoperative" (15a), both by repudiating it in principle and by ignoring it in practice, and then especially by accepting death under its impact on him because of his attitude toward this law. His resurrection was God's affirmation of the transcending of race antagonisms in the matter of God's relation to man and of man's relation to God.

Verse 15 goes on to say that the removal of this fragmenting wall had as its immediate end "that (in the Greek idiom) he might create the two in himself into one new humanity," thus "making peace." The larger concept, which must include the overcoming of group enmities and which really conditions the harmonizing of the human groups, is added in verse 16: "and that he might restore-in-reconciliation both the groups," now united "in one body, to God by means of the cross, having put to death the enmity by it."

The primary breach is between man and God. Being inimical to God and under his judgment, men antagonize one another, and humanity breaks up into opposing and conflicting self-centered and self-assertive groups. Enmity between God and men begets enmity among men. Self-centeredness and its self-exaltation and self-assertion cannot but produce rivalry, conflict of interest, antagonism, enmity. The cross of Jesus becomes the reconciling experience, the mercy-meeting point (Rom. 3:25) between God and men. "In his blood," as the atonement, and in their faith as the acceptance of reconciliation, God sets forth Christ Jesus as the "propitiation" between himself and men. Yet, as Jesus taught so emphatically on different occasions, including that of his "model prayer," men cannot be reconciled to God without being also reconciled to one another. So Paul here joins the two reconciliations as both effected by the Christ. Jews and Gentiles in him are restored to their ideal unity "in one body," and as one are "reconciled to God through the cross" whereon the enmity that slew him was slain by the superior force of love.

(3) Peace and unity now are preached as God's good news in the name and by the work of the Trinity (17-18).

In logical sequence, the Christ, having laid the basis for peace in this two-way reconciliation in his incarnation experiences, now "having come he preached-the-good-news (of) peace" to all on both sides of divided humanity, "to you, those who are far off, and peace to those near" (Cf. Isa. 57:19; Zech. 9:10). Peace with God is offered to both groups, as indicated by repeating the word "peace" with each group. After death, resurrection, and ascension, he came in the power of the Holy Spirit and entered upon the course of gospel proclamation through his believers. The glorious content and assurance of this gospel is found in the fact "that in him" who is our peace through the blood of his cross, "we have," as present and continuing privilege, "our approach, both of us ('the both' in Greek idiom) in (the) one Spirit unto the (one) Father." Redeemed man is thus linked with God in father-son relation in the sphere and activity of the Holy Spirit through the mediatorial Son. All the members of the Trinity are combined in securing our peace and securing us in the peace.

(4) The outcome of this reconciling and unifying work of God (19-22) is set forth in an amazing combination of thought patterns. Paul emphasizes that this grace of God working with the dead raw material of unregenerate humanity gives to the redeemed, as indeed even to God himself in relation to humanity, a new start. He begins the new paragraph with two Greek words (ἄρα οὖν) for which taken together there is no English equivalent. "So then" is too weak. The words almost say: "Note well the conclusion from all this." The conclusion calls attention to the high privilege given the saved, to the continuing process of God in his work in us; to the use God is himself making of the redeemed body of his people. It is all stated in the indicative

mode of continuing process but with strongly implied exhortation at every point.

"No longer are you strangers and visitors ('people not at home')" among the people of God's realm, "but rather fellow-citizens of the saints and even members of God's household" (19). Such is the status of all who have been made alive in the Christ and who now have our life in him. The saints all together constitute the commonwealth of God with individual citizenship. More intimately still, we are introduced into the family of God—one of the frequent teachings of the New Testament, which takes its rise distinctly from Jesus who taught his first followers to approach God, as he did, as Father. Paul says that God sends forth the Spirit of his one Son into the hearts of all who are adopted into the family "teaching us to cry Abba-Father" (Gal. 4:1-7). From every part of the New Testament examples will occur of this way of considering our experience in Christ.

It must not be overlooked that in all the section here the unity and oneness so stressed in the preceding paragraph are still emphasized. What each has, he has "together with (συν-) the rest—"fellow-citizens," "fellow-members," one compound word for each concept.

Our status is further described as secure because of our having been placed as material used in building upon the foundation of the apostles and prophets, the cornerstone being Jesus Christ himself. The general picture stands out clearly. Some details are not so clear. Are "the prophets," here linked with "the apostles," the Hebrew prophets, or the prophets of the Christian order? Either reference would fit appropriately into the picture. The characteristic function of the prophet is the same in both Testaments. It is to interpret what God is now doing in the light of his whole plan and work. By specific gift of revelation or inspiration, the prophet says: "This is what God means by this experience and event and what he says by way of relating this event and the people involved in it to God's continuing work and aim." We find "prophets" as important participants in the beginning and in the expansion of the gospel movement. Cases are too abundant to call for citation.

Paul may here very well have in mind, then, prophets both in the Hebrew Israel and in the Christian Church. The single article with "the apostles and prophets" suggests supplemental functions in co-operative authority and work and therefore specifically New Testament prophets. Paul's list of "gifts" of the ascended Christ for his continuing work in 4:11 (q. v.) suggests the same application. (Compare also at 1 Cor. 12:28.)

In what sense is the foundation on which we have been established as part of the building "the foundation of the apostles and prophets"? It can hardly be "the foundation which they are," as some would take it. That does not fit well into the genius and teaching of the Christian way of salvation. It might well mean "the foundation on which they also were placed," but this would almost certainly have been expressed differently. That it is their foundation as well as ours, in a possessive way of thinking, is true and congruous; but our status here is not presented as a possession so much as a condition. The sense seems to be "the foundation taught, and by their teaching laid down for us all, by the apostles and prophets." This means, in any construction, by the authority and in the truth of God. (Cf. 1 Cor. 3:10.)

The Christian status affirmed in verses 19-20 is no finished state, gives no ground for a *status quo* attitude. No, we have to advance in our citizenship in a growing commonwealth. We have to grow into the full meaning of our membership in the family of God. Character is a gift of God's grace that can be bestowed and achieved only in a process of growth. And we are taken over into the meaning and work of God in Christ Jesus "in whom every several structure, being harmoniously fitted (into the total architectural scheme) grows into a temple in the Lord."

The several buildings included in this figure of speech are the various race groups. Jews were first, then Samaritans, next Romans, Greeks at Antioch, and so one racial group after another, as the gospel was reaching out for all races. A great structure, like the Temple in Jerusalem and like temples to be found in all important cities, consists of many units, each unit with a relative completeness and beauty and utility. If the whole is an architectural success, each separate unit must be harmoniously constructed within itself and also fitted harmoniously into adjacent structures and into the total scheme. Paul saw the redeemed races thus, each growing into a temple in itself and growing into the total "temple dedicated ('holy') in the Lord."

So, addressing the particular group in mind, now in the grace and sphere and service of the Lord, Paul adds, "in whom you, too, in your turn are being constructed into a dwelling place of God in the Spirit." God as the Holy Spirit resides in his Church. That "God is in the midst of his people" is a constant form of Old Testament assumption and declaration. The Holy Spirit came into the Jerusalem church at Pentecost. In that first organized church he was also taking up residence in the Church. The consummation in the book of the Revelation is marked by the vision of "a new heaven and a new earth," and God coming down to earth with the New Jerusalem. And now henceforth

> "God's dwelling place is among men
> And He will dwell among them
> And they shall be His peoples
> . . . .
> For the first things have passed away" (Rev. 21:1-4 Weymouth).

Thus Paul rounds out his analysis of the Christian experience of the individual and of the social significance of the groups and of the total group, with this bringing together of these many thought patterns in which he seems struggling to impress the glory of God in his people whom he is producing through Christ Jesus. There is the one Body, constituted of the one new humanity. There is the one commonwealth of the ever-growing realm of God; the one household of the family of God; the one grand architectural masterpiece of redeemed humanity, incorporating units from all races, tribes, and tongues, and peoples. And all of it is glorious because it constitutes a holy temple for God to occupy in the Spirit. It is all built upon the Christ and all built in him in whom is all the fulness of the Deity. The analogy of Husband and Bride (see 5:22ff.) is not introduced here where it would interrupt the main emphasis. This section of the exposition thus comes to climax, as did the first section, with the complete oneness of Christ and his people for the glory of God.

III

GOD'S PLAN OF THE AGES TO ISSUE IN HIS UNIVERSAL GLORY—Chapter 3

Paul here reaches the widest meaning of the called in the Church and in Christ Jesus. Just as he followed the outline of the eternal purpose and its projection in chapter 1:3-14 with a prayer that the saints might sympathetically understand the glory of this purpose and their relation to it, so after his exposition of the individual and social experience of their calling for the glory of God, Paul here turns again to prayer that the called may fulfil their calling. In chapter 1 he makes a gradual transition from petition to further exalted teaching concerning the Christ and his Church. In chapter 3 he approaches his prayer (1), but turns off for an extended interpretation of "the mystery of the Christ"; of Paul's relation to this "mystery"; and of the universal significance of the Church for God's glorification before heavenly intelligences (2-13). He then returns to his prayer (14-21) in which he pours forth his soul in one of the most exalted flights conceivable in an inspired soul.

This whole passage baffles the grammarians. Findlay (*Expositor's Bible*) says it "is an extreme instance of St. Paul's amorphous style. His sentences are not composed; they are spun in a continuous thread, an endless chain of prepositional, participial, and relative adjuncts." It is one of the marvels of literature that this supreme composition seems throughout to be extemporaneous writing. Yet it is by no means "amorphous." A great soul, conscious of having received a most exalted revelation with which he had struggled for years to comprehend it, at length took an opportunity to try to write down what was beyond expression. His mind and heart, his imagination and all his powers of reason joined in the effort. He began, but always his subject was beyond words. He could point its dimensions in this direction and in that. Now exalted reason, now swelling emotion guided his expression. Prayer and praise broke in on his order of exposition, yet so far from interrupting its progress, advanced it and glorified it. Here in this Epistle with transcendent success he has set out in progressive outline that before which, in Romans (11:33-36), he could only stand in awed and adoring wonder:

"O the depth of resources, and of wisdom, and of knowledge of God!

How beyond research his decrees and beyond tracing out his ways!

For who ever knew the mind of the Lord; or who got to be his counsellor? (Cf. Isa. 40:13f).

Or who ever first gave to him and then got in return a gift from him? (Cf. Job 35:7; 41:11).

Because from him, and through him and unto him are all things!

To him be the glory throughout the ages. Amen!"

1. Approach to a prayer for the Church (1).
"For the sake of this" work of God outlined in chapter 2, and specifically for the sake of this uniting of all peoples through peace which God gives in Christ Jesus so that they are growing into a holy temple for his occupancy, Paul will pray.

"I, Paul, the prisoner of the Christ Jesus in behalf of you, the Gentiles," so he describes himself as the petitioner about to go to God. Whether as "apostle," "bond-slave"—his favorite title for himself—"chief of sinners," or "prisoner," always since he found that God had claimed him "to reveal his Son in me" (Gal. 1:15f.), Paul belonged to Christ Jesus. In all relations he took realistically and comprehensively what he says of us all in Romans 14:8: "Whether we live or die, we belong to the Lord."

Now that he is a prisoner for these four years, he is literally "the (not merely a) prisoner of the Christ," and it is "in behalf of you," specifically, "the Gentiles." It was by his standing firmly and vigorously for the full inclusion of the Gentiles within God's gospel of grace that he became a prisoner.

2. Explanation of "the mystery of the Christ" as preparation for the prayer (2-13).

At this point Paul breaks off. His readers may not even yet be prepared to say "Amen" with intelligent appreciation when he has made his prayer. There is still another thrilling aspect to this matter of God's universal purpose of grace. It is hardly correct to call this a digression, nor it is an "excursus." He desires to make sure that this prayer of his will enlist the full assent of his readers. Perhaps even yet they have not heard comprehendingly (accusative case) the range and reach of this stewardship of the grace of God which was given to him to be so administered as to incorporate them in its glorious task (2). He puts it with considerate delicacy: "If, indeed, you actually heard." The indicative assumes that surely they did—must have.

The commentators have found much needless trouble in this verse. How, they ask, can Paul raise questions about his readers having heard about his stewardship in behalf of grace for the Gentiles? The Christians of Ephesus, among whom he had preached and taught for three years, surely knew.

If we put ourselves *en rapport* with Paul at this time, we need have no great difficulty. He was, indeed, steward of a previously unheard of and undreamed of "mystery." He hardly dared hope that any fully understood it. His fellow apostles had been slow to grasp it. It had come to him with an amazement which he never lost even when the glory of his revelation convinced him that only in this "secret" can God be known. Christians all down the centuries have but poorly received it. The learned theologians and expositors of our own time either miss or hesitate over the terms in which the first apostle to the nations expounds his stewardship and pours out his soul in a prayer that reaches for the infinite and extends into eternity. The explanation and the prayer demand of us our utmost powers, a revealing insight and a more than rational boldness as we grapple with the mind of the eternal God in this revealing of his infinite grace.

(1) What is this stewardship (οἰκονομία) of God's grace? The grace, comprehending all the Gentiles, he has expounded in the preceding chapters. How that grace is to get over "into (εἰς)" all the Gentiles must also be understood if it is to succeed. "Grace given me" is always "on-its-way-unto-you." The translation of the King James Version, "dispensation," and continued in the American Standard and some other versions, has been given a meaning that is devastating to "the truth of the gospel." In its correct meaning it gives not the slightest basis for the so-called "dispensational theology" with which so large a following of godly people have been deluded. The term is never once used in the Scriptures, Old Testament or New, in the sense of one of a succession of "ages" in which God's principle of working with men changes from age to age. Nor is that theory of God in history taught in any other terms in the Bible.

The English for Paul's word here is "stewardship." It has this same normal meaning wherever he uses it. He wishes to make sure his stewardship of God's grace is understood, because it bears directly on his prayer, and on the scope of the gospel.

(2) That with which Paul was entrusted came to him by way of revelation in which the "mystery" was made known to him (3-5). He has already written somewhat of this ("in a little"; cf. Acts 26:29 for the idiom). The reference is to 1:9-10 and 2:11-22. He may be thinking, too, of other of his writings: Philippians 2:6-11; Galatians 2; Colossians 1:16-29 are suggested. "If his readers will read what he has said elsewhere, they will be able to sense his comprehension (σύνεσιν is the combining of ideas into a unitary concept) in the mystery of the Christ."

The term "mystery" was much used in the religious vocabulary of the day. A group of religions current through some three centuries made so much of it as to be treated as "The Mystery Religions." Their deepest truths were communicated to their devotees in very special initiation ceremonies.

God's great secret was his full purpose in his Christ in his incarnation, in his gospel, in his significance for history. (Cf. 1:9; 6:19; Col. 1:26; 2:2f.; 4:3.) This mystery is now revealed for all. It is not something recondite, difficult to understand. Rather it is the ideal, the inner purpose (here of God). This was something "the natural man" overlooks. It is not found out by research or by rationalizing; it is revealed (Cf. 1 Cor. 1:21-25.) This revelation Paul has had, so that now he knows what God's purpose is in the Christ. It "had not been made known to other (previous) generations, to the sons of men (i.e., to any part of the human race, not even to Hebrews) as now it has been revealed (aorist of definite, decisive act) to his holy (set apart in the interest of the new gospel function) apostles and prophets in the Spirit" (4-5). God moved "in the (Person of the) Spirit" to lay bare his inner purpose and ideal which apostles and prophets received, and could only receive and lay hold on, as they were "in the Spirit." It is "in the Spirit" that God and men meet and men come to understand God, in whatever matter and relation may be involved. When it is some matter in which the men involved are chosen as God's representatives to men generally, these men become God's interpreters and leaders of men in responding to God and doing his will. In the case in point these "holy apostles and prophets" were introduced into the most important of all God's "secrets," his real purpose and approach to the human race in his Christ, in Jesus his Son. Look again at 1:6-12 and couple with it the parallel, more condensed statement in Colossians 1:18-23.

As Paul has just said (3:4), when we face these and other similar words of his, we can discern the fact and the measure of his comprehension of this most significant of all God's secrets. We can understand, too, something of his humble, awed feeling as he speaks of "the stupendous grandeur of the revelations" (Weymouth) that came to him (2 Cor. 12:7 and the entire context in chapters 11 and 12).

(3) Now this great, deep secret out of the very heart of God—what is it? (6). It is not something for a select few, to be communicated to them by some exalted priest at the climactic point in a special initiation by means of some mystic sacrament.

It is, to be sure, the very center and source of God's interest in men; but it is what he desires all men to know. It is his open secret and so simple that the unsophisticated mind of even a child can see it and accept it in simple faith and trust.

Here it is, stated in three terms to make it as impressive as possible. "The Gentiles are jointly (with Jews) the inheritance" of God in the human race; "are (along with the Jews) within the Body" of Christ which is being created and grown in the Christian movement; "and are equal sharers in the promise (which is offered and to be realized) in Christ Jesus," the one mediator between God and all men (1 Tim. 2:5-7).

Attention must be called again to the term "inheritance," and to the fact that it is God's heritage in humanity that Paul has in mind in all his uses of the term in Ephesians. He intends to emphasize that God's claim of the Hebrews as his heritage was functional, provisional, and relative. In the gospel the distinction between Hebrews and "the nations" is abolished in favor of comprehension in the new Israel. Paul had at hand a term for "heirs" if he had desired it. We must use the term "joint-inheritance" because he did not mean "joint-heirs" in this connection. Each of the three affirmations is expressed in a single term compounded of the preposition *with* (συν-) and a word stem. In Romans 8:17 Paul speaks of all believers as "joint-heirs of Christ." There the text is *of* (genitive) not *with* Christ and, notwithstanding the translations, it probably should be understood as, *jointly heirs* of what Christ brings from God to men. Thus, the thought, though not the emphasis, is the same as here.

All this emphasis on the interest of God in Gentiles, as well as in Jews, may have little force for some readers today. It was intensely pertinent in the first century and has permanent relevance in the history of revelation and of redemption. It takes on relevance and emphatic significance once we see that the corresponding contrast for our day is between "Christians," who magnify "the covenant" consciousness and confidence, and "the heathen," whom we conventionally and sinfully regard as on a lower level in God's concern. We can make it concrete, and spiritually pertinent, if we say that God's gospel secret ("mystery") for us is that Chinese, Japanese, and Africans are in God's grace included in a glorious oneness with British, Americans, and Scandinavians.

The insistence has a further important relevance as correcting theories that insist that the Jews hold a preferred place in the regard of God in Christianity and constitute the determinant factor in God's control of history.

The Gentiles—all of them—come into this blessed relationship "through the gospel." Those already in this relation came by it in the same way in which those not yet included may enter it. So Peter discovered and affirmed in the Jerusalem Conference (Acts 15:11). Hence the urgency for preaching the gospel to "the whole creation," to "all nations," to "every man." All men must be given the knowledge of the Christ because they are all equally offered the blessings of God in him. The saved body will include all who accept the common salvation.

(4) Paul's personal function in this universal secret of God's grace (7-9).

Out of all he has said grows Paul's conviction about his own relation to this universal gospel, "of which," he goes on without break in his sentence to say, "I got to be a ministering servant (deacon, διάκονος)." His position in this was so important that it came to him "by way of and in the message of (δωρεὰν) a self-initiated gift of God's grace, which was bestowed upon me in conformity with the energy with which his dynamic will operates" (7). Paul's calling, position, and responsibility in God's enterprise with humanity was a tremendous fact with him: it made him a factor in the success of the plan.

Hence he will further define his call and commission (8-9). He is most modest about it. "Even to me (force of emphatic form and position of 'me' (ἐμοὶ), the less than least of all saints was this grace given." The comparative of the superlative form of "little" is rare and correspondingly emphatic. Paul could never get over his utter unworthiness of even the forgiving grace of God, to say nothing of being chosen most fully to interpret the Son of God (Gal. 1:15f). Here he appraises himself as lowest of all saints, not in comparison with other apostles. As a man, a sinner, the persecutor of the Church, he was "not worthy to be called an apostle," and on general principles was "least of the apostles" (1 Cor. 15:9). If insight, equipment, devotion, authority, fidelity were in question, although still accounting that "in myself I am nothing," he was compelled to claim that he was "not inferior to even the very chiefest of the apostles," as his detractors exalted them. Still, in the assertion of this claim in the interest of the Corinthian saints, Paul felt like he was "playing the fool" (2 Cor. 11:5; 12:11, and context).

His calling was for two functions (cf. also his claim at 1 Tim. 2:7): actually in his own person "to the Gentiles to bring the good news (of) the wealth of the Christ which is beyond all tracing out" (8b); and further to render the indispensable service of "throwing light on the stewardship of this deepest purpose of God which he had kept as his own great secret from the preceding ages." All the time, and even from before times eternal there it lay in the heart of God "the Creator of all things." Now it is God's open secret which he will have all men know.

It was—and is—necessary that the divine method for dispensing this glorious good news shall be known and accepted, known to all and accepted as the duty and the glory of all Christians. Alas, that they have been so little concerned with it. Paul was its first great interpreter and its supreme interpreter for all time. This was a part of his calling. Whether Paul was in this statement thinking of "causing all men to see what is the stewardship of this mystery" is not certain. The "all" of some versions, including the American Standard and Revised American Standard, is supported by some manuscripts but the balance seems to be rather against it. He was certainly conscious of his function "to throw light on the stewardship" (manner of dispensing—by no means "dispensational period") by which God would get his great secret made known to all men (9).

(5) The stewardship of that "gospel of the glory of the blessed God" (1 Tim. 1:11) is entrusted to the Church, is to be fulfilled by it and to come to completion in it (10-11).

God had held this secret in himself until "in the fulness of the times" he could make it known and set its stewardship in full operation "in order that now (at length) to the organized relationships and authorities in the heavenly realms and order the multiform wisdom of God might be made known" (10).

Nor was this use of the Church any afterthought with God; nor an adjustment to conditions of finite history and human failure. It was "according to a plan (laying-down-beforehand) of the ages which he formed in Christ Jesus our Lord" (11). The architectonic plan of the universe and the divine blueprints of all history God made around Jesus Christ as their central determining factor. And the carrying forward of these plans includes his becoming "our Lord," so that we become his Body, his Church.

(6) The proper reaction of a Christian to this surpassing concept of God in history, this using the Church as the continuing embodiment of his Christ, is indicated in verses 12-13. Paul's plurals here are probably in the first instance "editorial," expressing his own reaction. Yet they cannot but be the statement of what ought to be the reaction of us all. They do expressly include Paul's immediate readers (13).

At verse 12 we are compelled once more to part company with the commentators and expositors who support the popular, uncritical applications of the clause and its terms. The marvelous word of boldness in Hebrews 4:14-16, inviting us to approach God's throne unafraid through Jesus as our "great High Priest," is allowed to govern the reference of Paul here in Ephesians. The whole atmosphere and thought context of the two passages are different.

Paul has just been stressing the plan of God for getting hold on men for the glory of his grace by means of the Church. He is still moving in the extension of that thought when he says that Christ Jesus our Lord is he "in whom we have our (definite 'the') boldness and access by reason of our faith (which lays hold) of him." Because he is God's steward of the mystery of his grace; because he has assured faith that he is working in and in accordance with God's plan of the ages; because he thinks of all the heavenly orders of intelligence extending their knowledge of God by watching the advance of the gospel and the growth of the Church, Paul is bold to preach the gospel anywhere and to any person or group, as to the Areopagite court, to the assemblage of dignitaries with Festus and Agrippa, in "the household of Caesar." And he glories that he has access, gets a hearing, for his gospel. All this boldness and success derives from an unbounded faith in Jesus Christ and the power of God in his gospel.

Not only is he bold himself thus to preach and win. He will have his Gentile friends to share his feeling about it all (13). "Wherefore I beg you not to feel bad ('be-in-a-bad-way') over ('in,' when you sympathetically join me in) my afflictions (which have come to me in my devotion and concern) over you." Quite true, all these years of imprisonment and hardship had come about because of his espousal of the cause of Gentile standing with God; but "this is just your glory." What are the sufferings of one man in comparison with the glory of a world's salvation and God's satisfaction?

What a conception Paul brings of the plan of God and of the glory of the Church! Under its inspiration the world took on a wonder of meaning and the human race a dignity and glory of which he had never before thought or dreamed. And he has a part in it all! Of course, any tribulations we may suffer in such a context become for us "our light affliction, which is for the moment," because it is working out for us "heap upon heap an eternal weight of glory" (2 Cor. 4:17; Rom. 8:18). He is prepared to endure all things for the sake of the elect in order that they may get contact with a salvation which in Christ Jesus is eternally glorious (2 Tim. 2:10).

This had long been a definite attitude of Paul. Even if Paul's life is being poured out as a libation (cf. 2 Tim. 4:6) upon the sacrifice which he is making to God in bringing about the faith of the Philippians (or any other of the saints), even the utmost suffering that results from his preaching, and no matter what persecution may be incurred in his fidelity to his high calling, he can rejoice and congratulate those for whom his blood is spilled (Phil. 2:17). In it all he is only filling out in his body what remains to be borne of the afflictions of the Christ on behalf of his Body, the Church" (Col. 1:24).

And what a conception of the Church and its glory! Well does Findlay entitle a chapter amplifying 3:10-13, "Earth Teaching Heaven." "The magnitude and completeness of this plan are indicated in the fact that it embraces in its purview the *angelic powers and their enlightenment.*" "Christ's service," in the Church, "is the high school of wisdom for the universe." "The revelations of the latter days—the incarnation, the cross, the publication of the gospel, the outpouring of the Spirit—were full of surprises to the heavenly watchers." Yet, and this is of utmost importance: "It is not from the abstract scheme of salvation, from the theory or the theology of the Church that they get this education, but through the living Church herself" (Expositor's Bible, 167-173.) By proclaiming and extending the gospel, we help the universe to know God.

3. Now Paul returns to the prayer (14-21).

We must follow it in full recognition of the paragraph in which he sought to prepare us for it. We must be prepared for bold thinking, for largest vision, for deepest emotion. We are lifted above the limits of mere time and measured space. We kneel on a platform erected in the midst of the thought of the Eternal and the movements of his infinite love. Thus let us listen as Paul resumes, from verse 1.

(1) "The prisoner of Christ Jesus in behalf of you the Gentiles" (v. 1), on account of his relation to the age plan of God through his Church, "now kneels ('bend my knees') before the Father" (14). The God whose grace permits any man to address him as Father is all-comprehensive in his grace toward all men. Thus he is "the Father out of whom (as spiritual and ethical source) every (social grouping of men in) family (relationship) in heaven and on earth derives its characteristic name (as a family)." The word play on *patria* (πατριὰ) from *Pater* (πατὴρ) expresses Paul's conviction that men who are bound together in every sort of worthy social grouping derive the tendency and the ideal for such grouping from the original, archetypal, and loving principle of fatherhood in God (15). Paul's first thought

of families here probably was of the racial families which have so large a place in his thinking throughout this Epistle. From all these families of men, racial and every other, all who accept the grace of God are made members of God's household of faith. We all have our access through the cross to God as the Father of all and of each (2:14-19).

(2) To this Father Paul makes three petitions in behalf of the Church (16-19). Each petition is introduced by the same Greek conjunction, signifying both the purpose and the content of the prayer (ἵνα); but they are not joined by any connective, *and* or other. They are not co-ordinate but progressive. The objective of the first petition is found in the second, that of the second in the third. He prays for this in order to that, and for that in order to the final great end. They are all interlocked as the soul of the petitioner moves toward seeking the fullest satisfaction of God in his work of grace.

a. That the Church may be made the fit dwelling-place for the Christ (16-17a). My prayer is "that he will give to you, on the ground and scale of the wealth of his glory, to be made powerfully strong, through his Spirit (coming) into (and working within) the inner man, so that the Christ may take up residence in your hearts by means of the (your) faith."

This long clause must be seen in sections. The great idea is that the Christ must dwell among men to carry on his work of redemption and restoration. His dwelling can only be in the inner, moral and ethical man, in the hearts of men of faith. He must dwell in them first of all as individuals, but, as the one Christ, in his "fulness" his dwelling place will be in the united and integrated body of all believers—i.e., in the Church.

For any one of us to be a residence place of the Christ, we shall need to be made far more than normal human beings. We must be made strong, and that with might. The might is, of course, from without ourselves but is operative within. So Paul suggests that we must by dynamic operation (δυνάμει) of the Spirit, be made strong. This is the work of the Holy Spirit.

He comes into us for this purpose and carries on his work as he remains within us.

b. As the Christ dwells within his people and carries on his redeeming work by means of them, they will more and more come to know the infinite love of God which is personalized in the Christ, now living and manifesting himself within his people (17b-19a).

It is impossible with any sense of certainty to determine the grammatical connection of "being rooted and grounded in love." Is the phrase "in love" to be construed with what precedes or with what follows it? Its location in the Greek text, before "rooted and grounded," would normally leave it with the preceding clause, "the Christ to dwell in your hearts in love." But if the fact is to be emphasized that only by being rooted and grounded in love can we have these high and holy experiences, "in love" would fittingly precede these words. It makes good sense and expresses true relation of ideas either way, and either way it has full grammatical justification. We must be rooted and grounded in love to have the experiences and to enjoy the comprehensive insight called for in the sentence and the context.

There are further questions about "rooted and grounded." To begin with, is the nominative case of the participles. If they look backward, they would be expected to be in the genitive to agree with "*your* hearts." If the nominative case is to be explained as syntactically correct, the words will qualify the "you" as subject of "may be strong." In that case they would normally follow the *that* introducing the verb of the prayer. The arrangement can, however, be explained as a means of emphasizing each idea in the thought by forcing attention to each because of its unusual location in the sentence. This seems to be the best construction. Still, to throw these words "in love being rooted and grounded" into the midst of a long, involved sentence, in the "nominative absolute," would be an accepted means of stressing the importance of personal appreciation and response of the believers to the divine working in which we are included.

Once more the question is raised, in what love are believers rooted and grounded? Every possible answer has been proposed and advocated: God's love, Christ's love—for us, for all races, for humanity, for the Church, etc.; our grateful, responsive love for the Church in all its members and parts, for Christ, for God, etc. All these are legitimate approaches. Or is it, as suggested by some, the general principle and emotion of love which is the basis of all unity, strength, and progress in personal relations, as between God and men and men in relation to one another? In the family of God—here the master concept of the prayer—love is the root of vitality, the controlling motive, the force of unity, "the bond of perfectness," as it is called in Colossians 3:14 in a connection which closely parallels the general tenor of the Ephesian passage. We are then to be "rooted and grounded in the experience and principle of love" as a preparation and condition of understanding the transcendent love of God expressing itself actively in Christ Jesus.

It requires both figures "rooted" and "grounded," to convey the absolute essentiality of this basis of our relationship. We need not trouble over the "mixed metaphor" nor follow the tortuous arguments of the grammarians concerning the measure of Paul's consciousness of the etymology of the words as he used them.

Here then, at length, is the second phase of the prayer: "that ye may be adequately strong fully to comprehend, along with all the saints what is the breadth, and length, and height, and depth, even to get to know the knowledge-transcending love of the Christ" (18-19a). This clause is tremendously freighted with ideas each too great for any single sentence. To "get-down" in clear, ordered comprehension the fourfold dimension of the love of the Christ requires, in the cognitive process, surely, supreme strengthening of all the powers of personality.

Only by being located in the center of the love will we see it reaching, infinitely in every direction. All these reaches of the divine love Paul sums up by naming the breadth of the love, extending to all peoples; its length, through all time; its height, to the very presence of the Supreme God; its depth, to the lowest condition of human need. No one person, nor any one group can alone grasp this love. Only in conscious relation and co-operative fellowship and effort of all the saints is the knowledge of the love of the Christ possible. Here is the locus of one of the most grievous faults and failures of the history of the Church. Only together can we hope to explore and find this love. It is essentially an experience in co-operation. This is a central emphasis in Ephesians, as it is in the passion of the Christ himself, especially as made known to us in the writings of John.

Even all together we can know this love only partially and progressively, for it has a quality and a magnitude that always surpasses, literally "throws beyond," our knowing. We are never equal to its full comprehension: we grow in comprehension by working together in pursuit of our apprehensions.

"The love of the Christ" is another phrase evoking much discussion in the effort exactly to define it. It must be the love of God expressing itself in the Christ through all the cosmic and historic processes of God. It includes the incarnation as the historic movement in the life of the cosmic Christ. It includes the Christ continuing as the love of God in the Church and in the gospel by which the Church lives and grows and brings the world to know God. Because God is love, the Christ is in the world, and "as he is, so are we in the world"—a truth which Paul and John alike bring to us in the name of Jesus Christ. (Cf. especially John 14; 17:13; Matt. 28:20; 2 Cor. 5:18 to 6:1; Col. 1:27; 1 John 4: 17.)

c. The petitions come to climax in the third: that the Church may fully express the full intent of God in human history (19b). Here again the becoming hesitancy of our finiteness has combined with an incurable tendency to relate God's work in Christ primarily to its benefits for us, and so to hold the expositors back from following the bold apostle through to his true meaning in this final petition. Here he reaches the height from which there can be no beyond for the Christian imagination. The consummation of all the prayer is "that ye may be filled up to all the fulness of our God himself ('the God')."

We must go back to 1:23 for the terms and scope of this prayer. There, it will be recalled, the Church is the Body of the Supreme Christ, exalted as the head of the ordered universe, and specifically the all-inclusive and all-exclusive Head of the

Church. In this relation the Church is ideally "the fulness of him who is becoming the fulness of all things in all respects." He is integrating all things in heaven and earth in harmonious unity for the glory of God. All that is out of harmony and not ready for the integration he is redeeming through the blood of his cross. Thus he is fulfilling all God's intention in creation, providence, and grace.

In the realm of grace the Church is his creative product and as his Body it incorporates all his work and its results. This is, then, the prayer for the full realization of this ideal. The plural "ye," then, while intensely individual in its appeal and its responsibility, must be taken collectively. That one individual Christian should be "filled up to all the fulness of God" is inconceivable. Feeling strongly this impossibility expositors and translators, even RSV, have done violence to the Greek text, and substituted *with* for *unto*. They mean us to understand "filled with all the fulness of God's grace and his graces for the individual Christian." But that is not what Paul was pleading for. Only as the whole Body of Christ can the redeemed be filled "up to all the fulness of God." That is the goal. Here in this total, summary prayer are the processes and the stages in the complete significance of the Christ of God in history.

4. In the light of this supernal prayer Paul gives us his glorious doxology (20-21).

Lifted to the highest possible point of contemplating the work of God in Christ Jesus, and thinking of it in rapt adoration as a completed ideal, he calls his readers to a vast paean of awed glorification of God. A little particle (δὲ) ties up the concept of the doxology with the petitions of the prayer. "Now, to him who has the power, beyond every thing, to do far exceeding what we ask or think; (and to do it) on the basis of the power which is continuously working in us: to him (be) the glory in the Church and in Christ Jesus unto all the generations of the age (which includes and is the consummation) of (all) the ages. Amen."

Here we have ascription of glory to the infinitely effective God; which glory is to be in the Church and in Christ Jesus, each an entity but in the work of grace in history united as Body and Head. Church and Christ are to be looked upon by the universe as the unitary manifestation of grace in redemption. This glory is to continue endlessly, Paul combines the two most emphatic phrases for saying *forever*: "unto all the generations" and "unto the age"; and then amplifies by adding "of the ages." Then, for all to join him, the "Amen."

Explanatory comment can do little to clarify, certainly nothing to enhance this marvelous, complete doxology. God has the power (dynamic) beyond all things, and to use all things, for his purposes. His power is already and constantly (present tense) at work in us. It is a continuous energy working out an unvarying undertaking. The next stage in the Epistle will make explicit the powerful summons to us which this work of God in us holds. For the moment we give ourselves up to "praise of the glory of his grace." Our hearts recall this element of doxology coming continuously to expression in the course of the Bible record. Psalms 100 and 150 will link with the songs of praise "to him that sitteth upon the throne and unto the Lamb" in the Revelation, especially in chapters 4, 5, 15.

IV

THE GLORIOUS CHALLENGE TO THE CHURCH AS THE FULFILLING BODY OF THE CHRIST. 4:1-16.

1. The members of the Body are all earnestly summoned to full response to the meaning of our position in experience and purpose of our calling (1). The appeal is based on all the deep and wide exposition in the preceding discussion, "therefore" (οὖν). By a threefold use of the Greek word-stem (καλ-), which is the same as the English *call*, Paul enforces his appeal. Incidentally also he indicates by this means that in his own mind "the Christian Calling" would be one form for stating the topic of this entire Epistle. His connectives show that here he turns from setting his appeal in profound and comprehensive exposition to emphasizing and analyzing the appeal of the Christian calling in practical experience based on the reference of every part and aspect of Christian life to God's interest in it.

We must, however, avoid any sharp distinction between theoretical and practical.

We can reproduce Paul's play on the word call by a translation more literal than that in any of the versions. "I *call you along* (call-along for the Greek compound παρακαλῶ), therefore, . . . to walk worthily of the *calling* with which ye were *called*." The challenge feature is further emphasized by the order of words, the subject *I* follows the object *you*, call-along being the opening word. *Worthily* is also placed in position of emphasis.

Paul stresses his own relation in the appeal by adding the pronoun after the "therefore," and by recalling again that he is "the prisoner of the Christ in the interest of the Gentiles." While here he says only "the prisoner in the Lord," he refers back to 3:1 where the fuller description was used. Now that he is making his powerful exhortation, he is speaking "in the Lord," in his behalf, by his authority, as his representative. "To walk" here, as usual, includes the motive and purpose and acts of the whole content of living in social life, "Walking worthily of our calling" means that in all respects, within ourselves and toward all others, all actions are related to the meaning and purpose of our calling in the grace of God.

2. The spirit required for our worthy response is now set forth, (2-6).

(1) It calls for full, humble committal of the self to the interests of the Body in relation to all its members (2). All the members must be constantly "bearing one another up in love," which must mean more than enduring one another. This worthy walk will, then, have to be "with ('in the midst of') all lowliness and meekness" as to one's importance and relative standing; not demanding personal recognition or consideration but unselfishly serving. And when contacts prove irritating or discouraging, one's attitude and conduct must be characterizd by ("in the midst of") unfailing patience, longsuffering.

(2) The whole attitude and conduct will be under the principle of active, unremitting zeal for perfect unity of the Body (3-6). Here, still, for Paul the primary reference is to the entire spiritual Body; but out of this ultimate interest grows

most impressively the concern for constant, concrete application of the principles in the relations and contacts of the locally organic body.

a. The master passion, leading to worthy behavior, is "eager zeal ('being eager') to guard (in your own purpose and effort and in your influence on others) the unity of the Spirit in the bond of peace" (3). The Holy Spirit is working within the entire Body and in each of its members to effect, maintain, and perfect the unity of the whole. Christians are called upon to unite with the Spirit and with one another to the same end. The constraining bond (συνδέσμῳ = bond-that-holds-together) is identified as "peace" (appositive genitive). Even while unity of the whole body is incomplete, if elements not yet combined in the one body are at peace within the scope of their experience, the work of understanding and unification can proceed. It is always an incomplete ideal, but we must ever be striving for it.

b. Paul grounds his call for unity upon a sevenfold ideal and factual foundation (4-6). The whole Christian experience and movement are based on these fundamental, factual elements, He uses no verb—does not say the conditions ought to be, or are. He throws them down before us one by one, with qualifying words for only two of the seven. We set them out one by one.

(a) "One Body": the one all-comprehensive spiritual Church into which each member comes as he is made alive (chapter 2:1-10) by the divine act of regeneration. All the redeemed are *de facto* within this one Body. There can be no other. This sense of oneness and its obligation must be carried over into the visible, organized church body. Here, also, and practically first of all, the unity must be zealously guarded.

(b) "One Spirit." Most expositors agree, after considering every possible interpretation, that Paul can mean here only the Holy Spirit, who is the vitalizing, energizing, enlightening, and guiding Spirit of the Body. This accords with "the promise of the Father," on the basis of which Jesus repeatedly directed and promised his disciples to send the Spirit upon them and by means of the Spirit himself to continue within them. This accords, too, with the nature and method of Acts as the gospel of the Holy Spirit, counterpart of Luke's Gospel of the Son of God.

(c) "One Hope." "Even as ye were called in one hope of your calling." We have already seen (at 1:18) that in this Epistle this is God's hope. God was not looking forward to different destinies for different peoples. He does not intend that mankind shall be permanently divided and separated by sectional and sectarian limitations. Certainly his ideal is not churches which disown each other and refuse the fellowship of unity and love in common relation to the One Head. God's one hope for all whom he redeems must become the constraining hope and principle for all the redeemed.

(d) "One Lord," who alone "died for all" and purchased for himself men out of all races and conditions of humanity. About this there could be no question in belief. Even so there must be no divergence in practice. He must be Lord of us all and Lord in all things.

(e) "One Faith." Here again, after much feeling about, all expositors come to agree that the apostle means the one believing experience which is common to all who come unto God through Jesus Christ. It is not one creed but one living faith that all share and by which all are drawn together. The Church is, first of all, on its human side, a fellowship of experience, worshiping God through the Christ in whom we have all put our trust.

(f) "One Baptism." Paul uses the meaning of Christian baptism as a ground of appeal for committal to sinless living—"buried with Christ through baptism into death, and raised to be alive unto God through Jesus Christ" (Rom. 6:1-11; Col. 2:12, etc); and for the unity of all believers in Galatians 3:27. There could as yet be no question of "modes of baptism," since these were unknown until later. Deeper than division over "modes," which are actually substitutes, is the differing interpretations of the meaning of the ordinance ("sacrament") of baptism. It is out of the departure from the original significance that variation arose in the act of baptism.

It is difficult for Paul's appeal for unity on the basis of the one baptism to have its legitimate force today because of the lack of oneness concerning the reason for baptism. It is this common significance of baptism for all that Paul uses in his appeal. Out of divergence and disagreement on this point have grown the efforts to give some other meaning to the term here. The only reference other than that of the water baptism that would be tolerable, "baptism in the Holy Spirit," is excluded here because the Spirit's place is already introduced as the second of the fundamental *Ones*.

(g) "One God" climaxes the list. He is described as "also Father of all" believers—not here of all men, for only the members of the Body are here under consideration. The Father God is now declared to have three relations to all. He is "the One over all, and through all, and in all" the Body and its members. Such is the extent of the declaration here. It applies to all the members of the Body and to all that pertains to them. For the relation of all things, absolutely, to God, we may compare especially Romans 11:36, and in relation to the Son, Colossians 1:13-17. In 1 Corinthians 8:4-6, Paul combines and contrasts the universality of God in relation to all things and in relation to all Christians. God is not called the Father of all things, nor even of all personal being. The designation is applied to "the children of God by faith in Christ Jesus," except in an accommodated sense; e.g., Father of lights (James 1:17); Father of mercies (2 Cor. 1:3). It will be useful to compare in this connection 1 Corinthians 15:24-28, as combining all aspects of fatherhood in one completed order.

By the sevenfold foundation of unities and the threefold relation of God the Father to all the people of Christ's Church Body, Paul makes the appeal for unity as powerful as it can be made.

3. Individual responsibility of each within the Body, (7).

The intense demand for unity of all within the one Body for the one great end of glorifying God in Christ carries with it an equally powerful insistence on the personal responsibility of every member of the Body. The connective here (δε) leaves the relation to be determined by the thought context, whether *and*, *but*, or *yet*, as required to express the interrelation. The individual is not to be lost in the corporate unity, but is to accept full responsibility to God within the fellowship.

Because of this, each one is equipped with an individual share and quality of the grace of God. The gift comes from the Christ himself, in his sovereign will and wisdom, and on the scale and in the manner of his unconstrained bestowal. Paul emphasizes that each member stands out distinct from all the rest in the mind and in the giving of the Christ; yet the purpose is in every case making each one able to contribute his part to the great design of perfecting the growing Body. "And to each one of us individually is the (his share of) grace given on the scale of the free-giving of the Christ."

We may compare here Paul's more elaborate, detailed discussion of "spiritual gifts" in 1 Corinthians 12. There he emphasizes the sovereignty of the Spirit in bestowing the gifts (charisms), all "as he will" and all for the same end. There, too, he stresses the one Spirit, the one Lord, the one God, just as in Ephesians. "The free-giving" is free in the sense that it is wholly within the heart and purpose of the giver. The recipient has no claim, and the giver is unhampered. That is the uniform New Testament teaching: the Christian experience, first to last, is "all of grace."

4. The gifts of the victorious Christ are brought to view in verses 8-13, with Paul's characteristic condensation of related ideas and background reference, which give the interpreter a wealth of material for study in the effort to reconstruct the thought forms of the apostle.

(1) The right and the purpose of the Giver of all the gifts (8-10) are approached by Paul by way of an accommodated use of a stanza of Psalm 68. "Accordingly (διὸ), it (exactly what subject Paul's mind supplied cannot be known and is not important) says:

'As he went into the height he led
Captive a band of captives;
He gave gifts to men.'"

The psalm extols God as the leader who has gone forth in a great campaign of victory in behalf of his people; has overcome all enemies; returns in triumph to his exalted dwelling place, where he will dwell forever. He returns with captives and gifts, which seem to be not only imposed tribute but eagerly offered presents from the kingdoms which he has reduced.

The words Paul selects from the middle of the song of exultation of their deliverer (v. 18) serve him well for describing the going forth of the eternal Christ to win the victory of grace over sin and rebellion in the earth and his returning in triumph to the position of power and grace at God's right hand. He either used a text of the psalm different from that from which our versions are made (the texts are various here), or he adjusted the original to his purpose, as he does in other connections. The chief variation is that in the psalm the Victor receives gifts, while in Paul's version the Exalted Christ "gave gifts to men." This is not a conflict, but an extension of the idea. He gave to men the gifts he had gained by his sacrifice and victory.

"Led captivity captive" has called for extensive discussion of a wide variety of verbally possible ideas. The grammarians have fully discredited the notion used by some preachers of the abstract principle of captivity being mastered by the Christ. "A band of captives" is the natural and fitting sense. Without going into the complexity of many efforts to identify the captives, a view is here given that seems to fit the movement of Paul's thought and to clarify some of the questions about the whole passage. In his incarnation ministry Jesus captured disciples who came fully to own his Lordship and to turn over to him the title rights to their personality and service. They were now his men and women. That process goes on continuously. He is continuously capturing sinners by his grace and converting them into glad servants of his kingdom. Paul was himself just such a captive of the ascended Christ. It is these who constitute his gifts to men.

This prepares for and fits directly into verse 11, where his gifts are men called and fitted for specified functions. It is in direct logical derivation from the words of Jesus in the prayer of John 17 about his men whom his Father had given him and whom he had won out of the world, whom he is in turn sending into the world on the same mission as the Father had sent him. Normally, now that he is going to the Father, he might wish to take them along with him. His "greater work" which he has inaugurated will go on by his leaving them as his representatives in the world. All the upper room conversations (John 13-16) had led directly up to this prayer. It is to be noted also that the third section of the prayer is for the full unity of all who believe and who shall believe, just as Paul is here urging the same full unity. And in both cases the further end of the unity is the glory of the Father in the fulfilling of the work of the Son.

In verses 9-10, Paul emphasizes the two aspects of effective incarnation of the Christ. He first came down into the lower (than heaven) parts—i.e., the earth. Then he "went up on high." The "went up" implies the prior descent. The notion of "descent into hell," "lower than the earth," must be rejected, certainly so far as Paul is concerned. The idea, even if it had any foundation, would have no place here. Because of incipient docetic theories, Paul is emphatic that the one who came down is the same one who went up. And there is a compelling reason for this. He "went up clear above all the heavens, in order that he might fill out all things," as he had undertaken to do. Recall chapter 1, especially verses 8-10, 20-23; and compare Colossians 1:15ff., 2:8ff., and the reiterated insistence throughout the First, Epistle of John.

(2) "And he (emphatic insertion of the pronoun αὐτὸς) gave" his men for the functions which would promote the end for which he had come down into the earth and ascended on high (11-12a). He gave them: "some (in the capacity of) apostles; some as prophets; some as evangelists; some as pastors and teachers"; all "with a view to the perfecting of the saints unto (such maturity and equipment and devotion that they would all be engaged properly in) work of service. . . ."

These classes of special leaders are for the service of the Christian movement considered in its entirety. The first two have to do with the extending inauguration of the work of the

Church in its earlier stages. They may be called ministers of the General Church, or of the gospel in its inauguration in each community. "Apostles" are missionaries in the stricter sense. The twelve were originating missionaries. Barnabas was another, then Saul (Paul), Silas, Timothy, etc. The primary idea is not of their authority. They had that, in the proper sense of authority in a movement that is a growing community of life and fellowship in service, not an institution. The fact that they were sent by the Christ to begin his work in new places and set it going was, and should remain, the characteristic of the "apostle." To begin with, all places were new to the gospel—Jerusalem surely.

When the gospel was preached in any place, divine guidance and direction in the new fellowship, its organization, its discipline and its functioning in its community would be necessary. It must in each place be made to represent the nature and spirit of the Christian gospel. This was the function of the "prophets" through whom the Holy Spirit gave his guidance and direction. Where new beginnings should be made, how to proceed in varying conditions, how to "establish" the work called for definite wisdom and leading of the Spirit. This came through the prophets.

The missionaries (apostles) and the prophets brought about one unitary group in each provincial city. They then passed on to new regions "for the furtherance of the gospel." Each new city church was the base for evangelizing the entire community which constituted a political, economic, and social unit and now became a Christian social unit. For this work, which in our day is called by various names—city missions, parish missions, regional missions, and so on—the Christ "gave evangelists." The term is used but twice in addition to this—Acts 21:8, 2 Timothy 4:5. Evangelists expanded what missionaries had begun in provincial centers while these went on to other provinces to start the new work there.

Those to whom is ascribed the complex function of shepherding and teaching were the primary ministers of the organized church, which appears in the New Testament as including all believers in a city and its related regions. They were permanent leaders in the churches.

That these various functions were not exclusively held by those to whom the several functions were assigned, and that the men were not limited to one function is plain as we read Acts and Epistles. Paul exercised variously all the functions, as did others. Yet to each one form of service was primary and characteristic. The form of statement here clearly implies that the same men were both "pastors and teachers." Yet no doubt some were pre-eminent in one function and some in another. That they were not fixed "officers" or "offices" and in no sense "orders of the ministry" in the Church as an institution is clear from other lists, as especially in Romans 12 and 1 Corinthians 12. Christianity was not intended to be primarily or essentially "a church." See more fully pp. 56-59, 72-79.

(3) These functional ministries were designed to articulate all the saints in mature development for the work of service. The term "deaconship" ("ministering" or "ministry" in most versions) in its general sense is the descriptive word. Even this service on the part of all the saints had the further and ultimate end of building the Body of the Christ up to its complete fulness (12b-13). This is kept before us as the constraining objective throughout. The perfecting of the Body is the work, not of "the ministry" but of "all the saints," and the ministers are to prepare the saints for this work. "Deacon" never in the New Testament came to be a purely technical term. Christ is even called a deacon in Romans 15:8 (Gk).

The goal of all this is set out in verse 13 with an exaltation that few seem able to envision. The Body is to be built up "until we arrive, all of us together (the all in co-operative unity) at the (ideal and divinely intended) unity of (the full experience and exercise of) the faith (of believing union with the Christ) and (the unity attainable in and by means of) the accurate knowledge of the Son of God." When we attain unto that ideal, the whole Body together will have attained unto mature manhood (a man complete, ἄνδρα τέλειον), (even) unto the measure of the stature of the (very) fulness of the Christ." The Christ will have achieved his ideal fulness in his Church Body, will be complete (cf. again 1:21-23). The idea can only be expressed in its full content by the daring phrase "the measure of the stature of the fully grown Christ."

5. Full co-operation of all for this glorious end of the complete Body of the full-grown Christ is the challenge with which the final part of this supreme passage comes to climax (13-16). It is the most daring concept of the New Testament. We follow it with most reverent awe.

(1) We must hold before us as part of this section the transcendent goal of verse 13 while we see some details of the undertaking and the spirit of our participation in it.

(2) There are hindrances within us, as both the material for the Body and builders of the Body, each in his measure (14).

The work involves that we shall set ourselves wholly to it "in order that we may be no longer babes, (no longer) carried about on tossing waves and blown hither and yon by every wind of doctrine (that may come along, teaching no more stable and reliable than one may see) in the dice throw of the (mere gambling) men, or (as subject to what event may show up) in the sleight of hand (performance) that promotes the cunning of deceit (on the part of exploiters)". Such seems to be the group of ideas which Paul's terms condensed in these very summary phrases. We hinder and delay the growth of the Body by our immaturity, our instability, and the gullibility which subjects us to deception of novelty, emotionalism, sectarianism of teachers that beset us and would exploit us. The warning appeal of Paul has its need confirmed in the failure of the saints all down the centuries.

(3) Over against the dangers and delusions that would hinder, Paul calls for loving loyalty of all in all things to the Head who is growing his Body in the life of the Church (15-16).

a. The purpose must ever be "that in all respects we shall grow up into him who is the Head." This requires "being true," faithful, and loyal, which we can do as actuated "in love," for him and for the whole process and for all involved in it, and only thus (15).

b. Next is emphasized that all the growth in every part derives from the Head, out from whom the vital supply flows throughout the entire Body.

c. Then it is pointed out that in the process all the Body is being harmoniously united and compactly joined together by every joint receiving and transmitting the supply for the growth, each several part with proper energy performing its functions.

d. Thus in the spirit and persuasion of love the Body accomplishes its increase unto the building (of) itself up. This part of the sentence is involved, with numerous terms and with some uncertainty as to word connections. The total sense is very clear. Its last word is love, the element and inspiration of the whole glorious process which issues in the perfect Church fully and perfectly integrated in the perfected Christ.

V

GLORY IN THE COMMUNITY OF THE CALLED—4:17 to 6:9

At length we come to the community of the saints in the midst of the realities of living in the society of this world—to the Church made concrete in the church in a local community. We come to it out of the sublime calling of the whole number of the redeemed, out of the glory of God in their calling and the glory of their relation to Jesus Christ and his meaning for human and cosmic history. The oneness of the local body of saints with "all who call upon the name of our Lord Jesus Christ in every place, their Lord and ours" (1 Cor. 1:2) is to be recognized by every church, giving it inspiration and imposing obligation. Each church has its own opportunities and problems, which it meets not for itself simply but for all the churches of every community and always in behalf of the entire Body of the Christ. The behavior of each community group of Christians has significance for the whole of Christianity.

Paul envisions such local churches living each in its this-world environment, and he defines the principles that must find expression in their living in their community contacts.

1. Each church is a distinctive community within the order, and the confusion, of the world (4:17 to 5:14).

(1) The Christian community must be ethically and morally segregated from the "heathen" world (4:17 to 5:12). "This, then, I say and I am witnessing in the Lord (with whom I am identified and who constitutes the sphere in which we Christians live and act) that you are no longer to conduct yourselves in the same manner as the heathen walk." Christians constitute a new type of humanity (2:15-19) and are a new world growing up within the old world. Each church is "a colony of heaven" (Moffatt) located here on earth, as Paul says of "all the saints in Christ Jesus that are at Philippi" (Phil. 1:1; 3:20). This passage, as indeed all the New Testament, calls upon "all the saints" to conduct-their-lives as members of this new humanity and worthily of God's high calling in Christ Jesus. They are here to make spiritual and ethical conquest of the earth which is to be incorporated within the kingdom of heaven ultimately.

a. The low ideals and standards of the heathen must be repudiated and abandoned in favor of distinctive Christian ways of living (17-19). The heathen way of living is described in its moral and mental degeneracy by a series of cumulative terms that include all attitudes of heart and mind and suggest the various stages of decay of ethical and moral sensitivity, as they interact in the surrender of personality to fleshly indulgence. The description here parallels the more extended description of the course of sin in the process of depravity in the first chapter of Romans. There the process of sin, interpreted as persistent resistance to God and departure from him, is portrayed as it is accompanied by a sinking of the moral nature from one plane of depravity to another until men, in complete defiance of God in his judgment of such indulgences, "not only practice them but go on to give encouraging approval to others who practice them."

Here the approach is different but the intepretation is the same, with the emphasis on the opposing course of Christians and on their responsibility to condemn the sins of pagan society by the purity of conduct in the Christian community. The "walk" of the heathen is "in the madness of their mind"—the moral insanity in which conduct follows unordered ideas rather than being governed by principle (17). And this is because they have "become darkened in the understanding"—their reasoning clouded; and this is combined with and caused by their having "alienated themselves from the life of God"—from God's kind of life which he offers to men and urges them to accept. This state comes upon men through "the ignorance that is in them," ignorance not of the evil in itself or of the laws of God and of human nature, but a sort of moral stupidity which prevents from seeing the full meaning of conduct. This ignorance persists in men "by reason of a certain hardening of their heart" (18) which goes on as men sin, making them more and more callous to ethical impression, until they get to be "such as, having lost moral sensitivity have given themselves over to impurity for positive practice of every kind of sexual vice with greediness" (19).

b. The Christian standard is found in the truth concerning the Christ as it is embodied in the life of Jesus (20-24). "But you did not learn thus (such conduct) from the Christ, if indeed you heard him (as Teacher) and were instructed in (the ideals and standards of) him, even as the truth is in the (personal life and teaching of) Jesus" (20-21). The Christ, in whom we have our spiritual life and into whose Body we are being incorporated, is to control our conduct and our standards in all relations. We learn from him, and in the curriculum of his character and standards is no license or leniency toward impurity. If any should think so, let him know that he was not actually learning the Christ. The truth as to the Christ and his will for us is found in Jesus, the Christ among men, in human relations.

Here is the true teaching of the social standards of the Christ for us: "that you are definitely to lay aside (aorist) your old human self as seen in your former manner of living, that old man which is in process of decay (brought about) in accordance with (the law of the working of) the natural urges (which are essentially delusions) of deceit." For while pretending to lead to the satisfaction of natural passions, these urges are actually leading to the destruction of body and soul (22). In the truth of the Christ, you learned that with this definite putting away of the practices of your former evil nature, "you are to experience-constant-renewal (present tense) in your mental inclination ('the spirit of your mind')" (23). And this new mind is to lead you "to clothe yourself with the new humanity which in accordance with (the character and will of) God was created (aorist, and compare 2:10) in the righteousness and the holiness which constitute the truth" of life and reality (24).

(2) That the Christian Body must live in mutual loyalty, love, and graciousness is the plea of the next paragraph (4:25-5:2).

a. Being "members of one another," Christians must "deal truly" in all relations. This is the basic principle which must control all at all times (25). "Wherefore," in pursuance of this threefold principle of the Christian experience: putting off evil, being renewed, and putting on new ways of behavior; and in carrying out in practice the radical difference between the standards of unregenerate human society and the standards of the community of the redeemed, "definitively laying aside" (aorist), as summing up the "old man," "all falsity, let each one of you consistently (present) speak what is true with his neighbor, because we are mutually members of one another." We observe here Paul's characteristic switch to the first person within the sentence, a mark of his personal feeling of oneness with all in the Christian experience. Before we will consistently, unfailingly "speak truth," we must definitely and finally "put away all falsity" in principle. Falsehood is a device of self-centeredness. Also, to be true, we must accept in principle our common membership in the unity of all in Christ. Of course the insistence on truthfulness among members of the Christian Body gives no warrant for its neglect in relations with the heathen. The basis for integrity is somewhat different there but no less compelling.

b. The contrasting "natural" and "Christian" attitudes in a number of basic relations are indicated in brief, staccato exhortations in verses 26-31.

In the matter of anger, to which all are subject, it is to be suppressed and restrained and overcome. "Be angry," as you will upon occasion, "and do not sin." Sinless anger is the mark of a moral nature under control of ethical love. So far as it is personal resentment anger is wrong and hurtful, however impulsively inevitable. But, "let not the sun go down on your passing (παροργισμῷ) wrath, and (by such self-control for the sake of your Christian responsibility) give no standing place to the devil," within your own personality. Neither then will the devil find in you an instrument for falsity within the church. The devil can work no real ill in any community except when he finds "place" in persons (26-27).

In the matter of property, which so extensively tests character, "let the one in the habit (present) of stealing no longer steal." The injunction applies to all forms of getting goods, or values of all kinds, by indirection and not by honest exchange. "Rather in contrast" adopting the Christian way, "let him (acquire by) toil, working with his own hands that which is good." All forms of thievery, in high and low relations, have these two base features: they seek to acquire the products of the toil of others' hands, and they are not concerned for the ethical quality of the product but only for acquisition. The Christian ideal is not getting for selfish possession but in order that "one may have (something) to share with the one having need" (28).

In the matter of speech (29), putting it very strongly by inverse arrangement of the parts of the sentence, and by the positive approach to a prohibition, the apostle says: "Every word unfit (literally 'rotten') out of your mouth let it not proceed." Even if it is formed in the mind, shut it off at the mouth. It will corrupt you less if not permitted to work its damaging power in others; and if shut up within because of the restraint of your good desires, it will in the end lose its tendencies. There is, "by contrast," the Christian way: "if there is some (word) good, with a view to building up some specific need (defect or lack), (give it expression), in order that it may contribute grace (God's blessing) to those who hear (your word)."

In all these matters, especially still thinking of speech, which expresses the qualities of the self—"and do not grieve the Spirit, the Holy (Spirit) of your God, in whose operation (within you) ye were sealed (as belonging to God) looking unto the day of (your full) redemption" from all evil and of your complete character as God's children (30; cf. 1:13-14). Strive always to act in your ideal character as a perfected child of God.

Going on to thought of the various stages of inner selfishness and consequent inner repulsions toward others, the exhortation continues (31): "Every impulse of bitterness, and heat, and wrath, and railing, and reviling, let it be definitely put away from you, along with every sort of badness." Now that you are regenerated by the Holy Spirit and indwelt by him in the midst of the community of the redeemed, you must avoid grieving him by any sort of evil action or emotion toward others within the Body of Christ, whose unity and perfection it is the Spirit's function to foster.

c. As completing this high appeal, Paul now urges the example of God and the sacrifice of the Christ in love to inspire and impel loving graciousness on the part of all Christians (4:32 to 5:2).

Paul's perfect psychological method is noteworthy in all this connection. He does not prohibit sinful practices by mere inhibitions. In each case he sets up strongly the high appeal of positive goodness. He produces no vacuum but enjoins yielding to "the expulsive power of a new affection" (Henry Drummond), the reciprocal love of God and man and its product, love of man for man. So in this climax appeal he exhorts, over against all these evil selfish attitudes and courses: "but make yourselves (get-to-be) in relation to one another helpful." The Greek word signifies capable-of-use. To this end the way is pointed out: "with a good disposition making yourselves instruments of grace to one another." The term calls for more than simple forgiveness. You are to be instruments of grace. And literally the Greek says "to yourselves," for Paul is following through the thought of all being members of one Body.

Here God is our examplar and the source of our graciousness. We are "even" to act "just as God in Christ made himself gracious to you." God determines and discloses his attitude toward us, in all our weakness and sin, in Christ Jesus. So we, now by his grace, being in Christ along with others who share his grace, are to behave in the same spirit toward all (30). "Being gracious" is more than "forgiving." It reaches back into the motive and attitude of which forgiving is an expression. It is so behaving as to prove a saving factor in the offender. We are specifically exhorted, "therefore make yourselves (get-to-be) imitators of our (the) God as beloved offspring (of his) (5:1)."

Taking the nature of God as standard, we are to take the way of the Christ as model and inspiration, "and order your lives among men in the atmosphere and constraint of love, just as also the Christ loved you and gave himself up in behalf of us (change to first person), an offering and a sacrifice to God (which was satisfying to God) as (it produced) a pleasing odor." Just as Jesus Christ in his love gave himself in our behalf and even gave himself up in death in our stead as the offerings and sacrifices were offered to God in the Hebrew system, even so are Christians to express love for men to the limit. The self-sacrifice of the Christ was pleasing and acceptable to God and brought us into our relation to him through Christ.

Note how Paul here switches to the first person—in behalf of us—when he reaches the heart of the sacrificial love of Christ. The deep personal emotion expressed in Galatians 2:20 was an abiding state of soul and comes to consciousness whenever he touches the death of the Saviour. He sees this attitude of the Christ as the true mind of every follower of his. (Compare here Phil. 2:5-8; Col. 1:24.) It is this glow of personal enthusiasm, of grateful participation in the grace of God that thrills Paul and that he would stimulate in all the saints.

(3) Sexual morality must be carefully guarded (5:3-14). This was a vital point and an urgent need in the pagan world

of Paul's day. It is hardly less so in our day. Indeed, the growth of sex immodesty, impurity, publicity, and the flaunting audacity of sexualism within this century is indication of deep decline in social morality. Sex corruption has had tragic encouragement in high places, centering in Hollywood and in the military administration.

Dr. Findlay, in *The Expositor's Bible,* a quarter of a century ago used Ephesians 4:17-19 as starting point for a paragraph deploring the low state of English morality at that time. In America today his descriptions and warnings are even more applicable, and need greatly to be taken to heart by all Christians. Dr. Findlay says: "By two conspicuous features the decaying Paganism of the Christian Era was distinguished,—its unbelief and its licentiousness. . . . the second of these deplorable characteristics was the consequence of the former. . . .

"The 'greediness' with which debauchery was then pursued, is at bottom self-idolatry, self-deification, it is the absorption of the God-given passion and will of man's nature in the gratification of his appetites.

. . . .

"Amongst the Jews whom our Lord addressed the choice lay between 'God and Mammon,' in Corinth and Ephesus, it was 'Christ or Belial.' These ancient gods of the world—'mud-gods,' as Thomas Carlyle called them—are set up in the high places of our populous cities. . . . Hard by the temple of Mammon stands that of Belial. Their votaries mingle in the crowded amusements of the day, and brush shoulders with each other. Aselgeia flaunts herself. . . . Theater and picture-gallery and novel pander to the desire of the eye and the lust of the flesh. The daily newspapers retail cases of divorce and hideous criminal trials with greater exactness than the debates in Parliament; and the appetite for this garbage grows by what it feeds upon. It is plain to see whereunto the decay of public decency and the revival of the animalism of pagan art and manners will grow, if it is not checked by a deepened Christian faith and feeling."

In America this revival of animalism has not yet been so checked. In deplorable measure, Paul's description of "the brazen impudicity of this time" as a condition of being "past feeling" is increasingly applicable to American society. "The loss of the religious sense blunted all moral sensibility." "There is nothing more terrible than the loss of shame. When immodesty is no longer felt as an affront, when there fails to rise in the blood and burn in the cheek the hot resentment of a wholesome nature against things that are foul, when we grow tolerant and familiar with their presence, we are far down the slopes of hell." Down that slope America has indeed slidden far. Paul's words in this connection call for most earnest heeding.

a. All forms of such social sin are utterly incongruous with Christian ideals and impossible in the kingdom of the Christ and God (3-5). "Fornication and every kind of impurity or sex greediness let them not even be named among you as is eminently (καθὼς) fitting for people who belong to Christ ('saints'); and (avoid) talk of indecency and silliness and subtly filthy speech, all which are unbecoming. Instead (of all such talk, let Christian speech be) thanksgiving." How much time is wasted in "small talk" and, what is worse, filled in with evil-minded chatter. "For be well assured of this: that no fornicator or unclean person, or sex-pervert, who really is an idolater (putting sex before all else) has any place in the kingdom of our (the) Christ and God" (5). Paul's very strong Greek arrangement cannot be reproduced in acceptable English idiom. It would be, "For this be recognizing that every fornicator, or unclean person or person of insatiable sex who is (thereby) an idolater, does not have inheritance in the Kingdom of the Christ and God."

b. Theories which would justify or excuse sexuality are utterly repugnant to God and subject to his wrath (6-7). "Let nobody lead you astray" about this matter, "with words empty" of truth and reason. "For (it is) because of these things (that) God's wrath comes upon (men so perverse that they are to be described as) the sons of disobedience." Disobedience is so much in their very nature that they must be called her children. "Do not, then, (permit yourselves to) become sharers with them," in vice and, by consequence, sharers in the righteous wrath of

God. The modern age is cursed with numerous such theories which both excuse and encourage sex indulgence in many forms, as being natural, necessary, or in any case legitimate, and involving no ethical principle. Paul's passionate concern is needed for our day as for his.

c. The conduct of Christians, who are "light in the Lord," must shine exposure and reproof upon all immoral conduct (8-14). The contrast of all this ethical and religious appeal continues. The Christian community is a new kind of society and is intended to be a medium through which the character of all society will be changed by the power of God's gracious love working through the redeeming Christ. The contrast must be clearly recognizable and steadily maintained. This is difficult because all members of the Christian Body are such only as rescued from the unregenerate, "heathen" body of humanity. We all bring over into the new experience and relation an entail of our sinful inheritance and habits.

We need to keep-in-mind (Ephesians 2:11) what we "were by nature even as the rest" (2:3, 11-13), and what now are our responsibilities and our resources "in the Lord." Paul renews that contrast in the paragraph before us, to apply it specifically to the function of the Christian community as the instrument of the holy God in a pagan society. Thus he reminds his readers that they must definitely repudiate and eliminate all these social sins, "for you were formerly Darkness, but now (are) Light, in the Lord." It is important that he does not say you were in the dark but now are in the light. In your nature you were definitely part of the Darkness of sinful depravity; now by the grace of God you are taken up into the essence of the Light and you function as such. "As children of Light live-your-life among men (walk about, περιπατεῖτε)" (8).

Here Paul inserts one of his side remarks. It emphasizes his injunction by introducing a basic principle. He does it in the figure of fruit-bearing, and in the rest of his sentence mingles the two figures of light and fruitage, as is not infrequently done in the New Testament, by Jesus and by his apostles. "For the fruit of the Light (consists) in every form of goodness, and righteousness and truth." The Light in you produces conduct that is characterized by the three basic attitudes and principles in human relations.

"Goodness" is the quality of truly integrated and balanced personality as related to other persons. "Righteousness" is the disposition and practice of what is right in relation to all persons. "Truth" is perfect adjustment of each person and all his intentions and acts with the ideal of the whole of being, so that one is perfectly integrated into the harmonious whole of God's character and purpose. This can all come only from the Light, through "the true Light that lighteth every man," and only as we become "children of the Light" (8-9, and compare Jesus in John 12:35-36).

Resuming his sentence, after the pregnant side observation which enforces his exhortation, Paul continues, reminding his readers that for their conduct as children of the Light they must be continually "learning-by-discrimination what is most pleasing to our (the) Lord" (10). That is to be the test of all Christian conduct. (Compare Rom. 12:1-2; John 16:8-11; Col. 1:9-13; 1 Thess. 4:1, etc.)

"And," living in this spirit and by this test, "have no sharing in the doings of the Darkness, these unfruitful doings; but rather positively (even καὶ) expose them" for what they really are, by the contrast between your behavior and theirs (11). "For the things that go on in secret among (under) these children of Darkness it is degrading even to talk about (12)." What they do openly may be condemned by conduct and by declaration: what they do in secret, too base to discuss, may still be rebuked by contrast with chaste Christian behavior. "And all things when tested by the Light are clearly revealed" for what they are: "for everything that endures full manifestation is (itself of the nature of) light" (13).

This seems to be the meaning of one of the most difficult phrases. The commentators and expositors have labored energetically and with exhaustive ingenuity to solve the problems of construction and connection. The translators have adopted various renderings. A word by word translation is: Everything for (γάρ, never first word in a Greek sentence) the made manifest light is." If "everything" followed "the made manifest," it could mean "the light when it is made manifest (by being applied) is everything"—the all-important factor in dealing with social sin. This is a new suggestion, in addition to the many already proposed. The rendering above is also specifically novel but fits the context perfectly and is lexically and grammatically allowable: "everything that endures clear manifestation is light." The rest of the sentence agrees with other expositors.

The appeal climaxes with a quotation, nowhere found in this form. It may be from an early Christian hymn already known in Paul's time. Paul's own summary phrasing presents the central idea found in such calls as that of Isaiah 60:1-3, 52:1-2; 58:8. We may compare Paul in Romans 13:11-14, 1 Thessalonians 5:5-11. It is one of his constant exhortations, as indeed of Jesus and of the New Testament generally. "For this reason," says Paul here, "there is the saying"—which we need no further to seek to define:

> "Rise, thou who art sleeping,
> And stand up from among the dead
> And the Christ will gleam forth upon thee."

By our faith in Christ we experience a spiritual resurrection and become centers of shining for the ethical illumination of social practices. "For God who said, 'Out of darkness light shall shine' is the one who set light to shining in our hearts with the purpose of giving the light of the knowledge of the glory of God in the face of Christ" (2 Cor. 4:6). And that light of God irradiating the face of Christ, by its reflection from us makes us "the light of the world." In that light men seeing our good works will glorify the Heavenly Father. Such was the plan of Jesus (Matt. 5:14-16), which Paul here follows.

2. The community of the called is one whose governing principle in all relations is "the will of the Lord" (5:15 to 6:9).

(1) This principle of living must be clearly defined and fully accepted (15-21). Consistent living is achieved only on fixed principles.

a. There is need for sharp discernment in this evil day (15-17). "Keep sharp lookout, therefore, how you order your lives ('walk-around'), not as (men) lacking in wisdom but as wise men." The Christians' motivation and their accessibility to the guidance of the Holy Spirit should give them an orientation and a discernment in social judgment and conduct which would mark them as wise in social ethics and superior in ethical standards and influence. With all their failures to live by the ideals of Jesus Glover's witness is true that the early Christians "out-lived, out-thought, and out-died" the heathen. It has been true through the course of history and is true today. But it can be far more true, and must be if the close-knit world of today is to be saved from degeneration and ruin.

Christians must still be alert for "buying up the opportunity" as it appears in the changing markets of human interchange. The opportunity in the current world crisis is vast, and if bought up promptly will yield enormous profit for the spiritual, the economic, the social good of all the world. An opportunity is on the market for advancing the kingdom of God immeasurably, if only the Church is discerning, prompt, and prepared to pay the price for so rich a pearl. But it requires quick action "for," still, "the days are evil," are full of danger for Christianity as for humanity (16).

The exhortation is for every age. "Because the days are evil," "on this account do not become lacking in thought, but discern-rationally what the will of your (the) Lord is" in every situation so that you may do his will on earth with each fleeting opportunity (17).

b. Peculiarly pertinent to the modern situation is the next injunction: "Especially (force of 'and' here) do not get muddled up with wine, in which is gross insecurity." Men do need some stimulation and inspiration in times of depression, disappointment, grief, failure; and even when the drabness of routine living oppresses the spirit; as also in times of joy and gladness. In all such experiences the Christian gets his lift of spirit not by the muddling confusion of alcohol which leads to "riot" and "excess" and "unsafety"—indeed to every sort of crime and vice. His resource, "on the contrary," is to "be filled with the Spirit." Literally it is "in the Spirit." We live in his environing and by his control. When occasion requires, we may have a fresh "infilling" of his grace so that we will come into "fulness" according to need and occasion (18).

There is a vast difference between muddling up the resources within oneself and receiving new resources from the Spirit of God. With this resort to the Spirit, we express our enthusiasm or victory, not in harmful excesses but by "speaking to one another (literally 'to ourselves,' in group unity) in psalms of praise, and hymns of joy and odes inspired by the Spirit and recited under spiritual impulsion." Thus we shall be "singing and offering praise in our (your) heart to our (the) Lord" (19). And we shall be "giving thanks always over all things to our (the) God and Father, in the name of our (here Paul definitely switches to first person) Lord Jesus Christ" (20).

Thus in all our unusual experiences of special need or of triumph, we maintain the consciousness of wider connection, of divine relationship of dependence and fellowship. Our God is our Father as we approach him in his Christ, our Lord with whom we are associated in his human expression as Jesus. In him we live with God as Father and so make every experience holy. In that consciousness we can never wish to give ourselves to any form of dissipation for hilarity or for benumbing forgetfulness.

c. And now for the constraining principle to which the whole paragraph applies. All members of the Christian community will live and act on the principle of "subjecting ourselves to one another in reverence for Christ." Here the reading is not "to ourselves," as in verse 19 where it is collective, but "to one another," distributively. And the participle is in the middle voice, leaving each individual autonomous and responsible. The subjection is to be voluntary, personal, having full ethical value for the one who subjects himself and for the others whom he serves in spiritual surrender (21). The obligation is imperative and universal. It is a principle for collective living. It at once gives the constraint of divine control, preserves the autonomy of the individual by which alone free personality is developed, and achieves the responsibility of ethical values in a corporate society.

(2) Applying the principle in the basic relations in the economy of the family household (5:22-6:9). With no grammatical transition, and with no particle to indicate the logical transition, Paul passes on to the specific application of the principle of subjection in the Lord to the three structural household relations:

a. The relation of husband and wife is first (22-33). The participle, "subjecting yourselves," of verse 21, where it has universal reference within the Christian community, is now, without being repeated and with no finite verb, applied to wives. This gives the grammarians some trouble. The majority of manuscripts supplied a finite verb, but with no agreement among them. The group of manuscripts lacking it must be accepted as correct. Paul's comprehensive, clear-thinking mind, with its passion for thought continuity, found no need for repeating his great word of subjecting yourselves in a finite verb form just for grammatical fulness; and the remarkable flexibility of the Greek language with its syntactical paraphernalia enables the reader and the hearer to follow his mind which so easily carried the parts of almost unending sentences without losing their proper relations.

(a) There is really no grammatical difficulty, then, in seeing "the wives ('subjecting themselves'—from verse 21) to their own husbands in the Lord" (22-24). All that Christians do is, in Paul's way of thinking, done "in the Lord." What most Christian teaching through the centuries has missed in using this scripture is that the wives are not "commanded" to accept subjection to husbands, but are enjoined to "subject themselves." The initiative, the autonomy, and the practice are all left with the wife. It would have to be so in the Christian economy. How could it be otherwise in a religion founded by Jesus? In him as the Christ there "can be no male and female," for we "are all one in Christ Jesus" (Gal. 3:38). Christian husbands must keep the prayer way to God's presence open by "dwelling with their wives on an intelligent basis, giving honor to the woman as (physically) the weaker vessel, but as being also joint-heirs of the grace of life" (1 Pet. 3:7).

For the first time in human history men and women, in the religion and the Church of the Christ, were put on a basis of equality in worth, in grace, in privilege, where each according to fitness and spiritual gifts was to find and fill the appropriate and effective function for the growth of the Body of Christ.

Jesus' attitude toward women appears in the record as a matter of course. It is not justified or defended. He simply did and said what was right and left it to be accepted and applied. It was not his way to support his teachings by argument or appeal to authority beyond his own words.

Into a world that subordinated, depressed, degraded, and exploited women came Jesus with his clear-visioned humanity. Through the revelation of God in Israel and the prophets of God to Israel, a path had been opened which he straightened and widened to make it a highway of honor for women and for men and women as together they should walk the way of the kingdom of heaven.

This ideal of Jesus and practice of the early Church has not had full expression in any social order nor in the Christian churches in any period of their history. In the New Testament this was not set forth as a demand nor as a dogma. The oppressed and suppressed elements of society were not taught or encouraged to go forth crusading for rights. Christianity calls upon its followers to serve, not to assert themselves; to proclaim God's grace for all, and themselves ever to be bearers of blessings to others. Through the centuries Christian women have witnessed and served and waited on God to enlighten Christian men concerning their place and capacity in Christian institutions.

The Christian church arose in a man's world and its men thought largely in terms of masculine responsibility and dominance. The Christian movement has expanded through the centuries into regions and cultures which were controlled by men who subordinated and dominated women. Thus almost universally men have applied and women have accepted in the churches the social standards and conventions of the communities in which the churches arose. This they did almost unconsciously and in this, as in so many other matters, did not seek to find and express the mind of Christ or give freedom to the genius of the Christian religion. Very naturally and inevitably men were the interpreters of the terms of the New Testament and expositors of the Christian principles. A too masculine cast has been given to the interpretations and expositions. Jesus Christ has not been thoroughly understood nor has his mind found full expression in the polity and procedure of his churches.

All translations of the Christian Scriptures reflect the warped viewpoints of man-controlled institutions in passages dealing with women, and the established interpretations further misrepresent the meaning of the original words. The most glaring example of this is the passage in Ephesians 5:22-32. The Authorized Version reads, verse 22, "Wives obey your husbands, as unto the Lord." There is no imperative form in the Greek. The word does not mean obey. Furthermore, the voice of the participle is not active or passive, but middle. It carries an exhortation to women in the disposal of their own lives. The autonomy of the wives is left with them, and the responsibility for their behavior is left with the wives.

In the two succeeding paragraphs, in chapter 6, we do have the word "obey" in the imperative mood of a verb that places the authority in the parents over their children and in masters over slaves. ὑπακούετε means "hear" as a subordinate and carry out the will of another who has right to command.

Wives, in the autonomous responsibility for their own conduct under God, are expected to order their lives in voluntary adjustment to their husbands as rightful head of the family. This perversion of grammar, syntax, and sense has become "law" instead of gospel and has found place in the approved marriage ceremony of the sacramental churches from which most of the democratic churches have borrowed it.

In the American Standard Version, we find twelve verses, with thirty-eight lines, enjoining reciprocal duties on wives and husbands. Here, men being the expositors and preachers, it has come to be generally understood that the major emphasis is on the duty of the wife, and often it is wholly ignored that the husband comes in also for instruction. Now the fact is that 3 verses, 8 lines, are devoted to wives, while 8 and 2/3 verses of 28 lines emphasize the Christian standard for husbands; with 1½ lines at the end usually applied to the wives, but requiring the supplying of two verbs to give that interpretation. Worse still, there is not an imperative verb applied to the wife, but the husband is laid under an imperative supported by several lines of argument.

The wives, then, are to see the true significance, order, and symmetry of the family in a Christian society and so to take their place and so demean themselves as to constitute truly Christian families and to commend Christian ideals and standards as worthy of the grace of God in Christ Jesus. They will subject themselves to their own husbands (21) "because," in God's plan for the family, "the husband is head of the wife, even as the Christ is Head of the Church—in his case Saviour of his (the) Body" (23). The relations in principle and in general are the same; but the Christ holds a unique relation to his Church in that he is its Saviour, its Creator, as man is not, of course, in the same sense for his wife.

This appeal to the wife is heightened by asking her to make the Church's relation to her Christ the ideal for the wife in relation to her husband. Even though the husband can never be in the same creative sense her head as the Christ is Saviour-head of the Church, "still (the sense of ἀλλὰ, but, here) as the Church arranges her existence and activity in subordination to her (the) Christ, in this same way are the (Christian) wives (to relate themselves) to their (the) husbands in everything" (24).

(b). Now for the ideal for husbands (25-31. They must relate themselves to their wives as the Christ relates himself to his Church. This is enforced in a series of imperatives and comparisons and is characterized by great earnestness and tenderness. "You (the) husbands, love your wives even just as (καθὼς καὶ) the Christ loved his (the) Church." The same high word for love is used of both the husbands and the Christ. Perhaps we may not quite see why Paul does not say that wives are to love their husbands. Was this taken for granted? Or was it that the ideas of the ancient world, with the restrictions on woman's freedom, had not yet risen to selective, discriminating love as to be expected in women? This word "love" (ἀγαπὴ) used here could reach downward, e.g., God toward men, or outward on a level, not from a subordinate conscious of the subordination.

How, and how greatly the Christ loved the Church is shown by adding "and he gave himself up (unto and in death) in her behalf" (25). This attitude of the Christ, now so strongly urged upon husbands, is utterly unselfish, is not merely emotional, has direct and ultimate aims. It relates to the interests of all the scheme of grace. The family is within the divine community and should take its nature from the context and significance of the inclusive Christ-Church entity. Thus the Christ "gives himself up in the interest of his Church, in order that he may sanctify (set apart wholly) her, having purified her by the bath of water, as the saying has it" (26).

Extensive struggle and research have led expositors to no secure understanding of this unusual figure and its terms. There is probably a general reference to the baptism symbol, although that is by no means certain. The use of the bridal bath is manifestly the source of the reference, and it is quite possible that Paul did not think through the analogy but used it in a general way. Efforts to work it out in detail are futile and useless. Some read back into Paul's words a sacramental significance foreign to his thinking. The spiritual, ethical cleansing of the Church, as of each of us within the Church, is not a single event effected in a physical act. It is the fact of purification Paul is insisting on here, not its method. Hence the appropriateness of understanding (ἐν ῥήματι) "in a word" to suggest "as the saying is."

More specifically, and looking to the ultimate goal the purpose is "that he may himself present his Church to himself glorious (as his Bride), not having a spot or a wrinkle or any of such defects, but (his purpose is) that she shall be holy and without any thing to find fault with" (27).

We must not permit questions of analogy and syntax, nor even any supposedly new teaching concerning the Christ and his Church to divert us here from the main emphasis of the passage. The Christ-Church relation is assumed: its details so far as introduced here are for enforcing on husbands their duty of holy and helpful devotion to their wives in the interest of a perfect union, a sacred family, a worthy unit in the Christian community, and satisfying to the saving Christ.

"Thus (as the Christ his Church) are husbands, too, under obligation to love their own dear wives as (they love) their own bodies." This is, in the true light, no exaction and demands no sacrificial strain, for in "loving one's own wife he is actually loving himself" (28). It is put this way "because no one ever hated his own flesh; on the contrary, he feeds it and nourishes it, just as the Christ also (feeds and nourishes) his (Body, 'the') Church" (29). This concept of the Church as the Body of the Christ is appropriate "because as members we constitute his Body" (30).

Corresponding to this conception of the way husbands are to think of their wives and conduct themselves in relation to them, and supporting this conception is the original ideal, recorded of the first union in Eden, strongly reaffirmed by Jesus (Mark 10:4). "For this reason"—in view of God's command and the fundamental concept of marriage and the family, and of God's purpose in human society, as well as of the ideal in the Christ and the Church—"a man shall leave behind (lay down the relation to) his father and his mother and be definitely united with (etymologically, 'glued-to') his wife; and they shall become, the two of them, (into) one human unit" (the implication of "one flesh)" (32).

The major emphasis in all this is placed upon the husbands, because in the society of all Bible times laws and customs assumed the autonomy and freedom of men, but assumed subjection and submission in women. Women did not divorce husbands nor leave them, except as "put away" by them. Christ for the first time in history gave to women their freedom, autonomy, and integral value in society. Woman became a person under the touch of the hand of Jesus.

Centuries have not been sufficient for society, not even for the Church, to accept and work out the implications and applications of this emancipation. Women were sure to make mistakes themselves and to assert their freedom in ways detrimental to social good and Christian progress, even as men have done through the ages. In our modern world we are in the midst of the confusion of immature transition to Christian freedom in the marriage relation. Self-assertion on the part of women clashes with the selfish domineering of men, and adolescent individualism, lacking the constraint of Christian love, is playing havoc with marriage. Families are too often wrecked by sinful selfishness, or continue in wretched disharmony. Not "subjecting themselves to one another in the fear of the Lord" men and women profane the sanctity of the holiest human relationship with conflicting selfishness. Failing to seek the glory of God in marriage sanctity, they shame humanity with the violation of marital ideals. Only "in the Lord" can marriage be worthy.

(c) This high standard is most emphatically urged upon Christian husbands and wives (32-33). "This divine ideal is great: yet I say, up to Christ and up to the Church" (32). It is a striking witness to the failure to grasp the direct purpose and force of this passage that marriage ceremonies through centuries have declared that "God in his Word has made the relation of husband and wife the symbol and ideal for the relation of Christ and his Church." It is exactly the other way about. He sets up the assumed perfect relation of Christ and Church as ideal and standard for husband and wife. Paul fully recognizes that the ideal he has presented is difficult for human acceptance, even for Christians to grasp in its full significance. When Jesus set up the same standard, even his disciples thought it impossibly high (Matt. 19:3-12).

As for the meaning of the passage here, recall the discussion of "mystery" at 1:9; 3:3ff., where it was shown that it means

"God's revealed ideal." Then note the emphasis on I in the Greek text. Note also that the preposition (ἐις, "into" or "concerning," etc.) is repeated with both Christ and Church, showing that they are to be taken distributively. Most translations render the phrase, "I speak concerning Christ and the Church," or some similar statement. Now Paul was not speaking concerning Christ and the Church but concerning wives and husbands. He introduced Christ and the Church to illustrate and to set the ideal. No Greek scholar, if given the English sentence as it stands in any of the versions to put into Greek, would ever produce the Greek of this passage (ἐγὼ δὲ λέγω εἰς χριστὸν καὶ εἰς τήν ἐκκλησίαν). "Concerning" is not the equivalent of the Greek preposition here. It is not easy to see how the rather obvious meaning has been so generally missed. The *Expositor's Greek Testament* explains the separate items correctly, with much elaboration, and seems to be coming out on the real meaning, then fails at last.

Taking the sentence in its preceding and following context, and following the natural Greek construction, we have Paul recognizing the difficulty of his standard and then reaffirming it with emphaiss: "This revealed ideal is great; but I (still) say, up to Christ (on the part of the husband) and up to the Church (on the part of the wife). Furthermore, do you, for your part (καὶ), each one individually, love his own wife as himself; and the wife let her respect her husband." With that emphatic restatement he leaves it. The final word as to the wife is introduced in a subjunctive, purpose (or intention) clause, not imperative as in the case of the husband; thus leaving the primary responsibility upon the husband.

b. The relation of parents and children naturally follows, (6:1-4).

(a) "The children" are addressed. Then their duty is stated in the imperative of a word meaning to hear and obey (ὑπακούετε —hear as under another). As with servants and masters below, the initial and authoritative will is in the parent. The child's will is to be an extension and executive of the superior will. It is not as in the case of wives, whose will is autonomous and free. They decide what is right and will to do it. In the parent-child relation the parent decides and wills, while the child wills to do as directed.

"Be obedient to your parents." Whether the text includes "in the Lord," as in Colossians 3:30, with a different arrangement, is not certain. There is no question of Paul's attitude, however. His added reason implies it: "for this is right" (1-2), in the sense of righteous conduct, not merely what is humanly appropriate. He enforces his charge by quoting the commandment: "Honor thy father and thy mother, which (specific commandment) is primary (for children and is set) in a promise: in order that it may come to be well for thee and thou mayest be of long continuance upon the earth." Paul somewhat generalizes the content of the promise of Exodus 20:12, to give it its universal Christian application. The futile effort to explain this as "the first commandment of the Decalogue with a promise" is avoided by the natural and true idea of "primary" for children and carrying God's "promise" of enduring good life (3).

(b) Of course, the command to the children in the Christian family persupposes intelligent, devoted Christian parents. It is a grave and holy responsibility to make our wills the directing authority in our children. It must be used to develop moral judgment in our children and capacity for autonomous ethical willing in them. In due course obedience to parents must issue in responsible voluntary co-operation and then in fully autonomous self-control. Paul does not leave this—here or in the Colossian parallel—to inference. He begins with prohibiting a too prevalent sin. "And you parents (fathers), do not irritate your children" by wrong methods and spirit in their control; "but rather nurture their growth (nurture them out) in child-culture and mental development with reference to the Lord" (4). It is not easy to express this genitive "of the Lord." It is the training and personality development that the Lord desires them to have, and that is imparted in the consciousness of him and of his intent. The education which is of the Lord relates all phases of it to the Lord.

c. Relations of masters and slaves (5-9).

(a) Characteristically Paul leads the slave to go beyond all incidental, temporal, and artificial conditions, limitations, and controls and to think of himself as a Christian soul related first of all directly to his divine Lord. Then through all the media of human arrangement he will serve his Christ, who deals with his servants on the same principles, whatever their human social status, "whether slave or freeman" (8). His first word might seem to call on slaves to accept their status in full submission and so to sanction the *status quo* and to put Christianity back of the system of slavery. Before Paul finishes his brief paragraph, he has enunciated principles which must in time destroy the system of slavery, not by social or political revolution but by ethical and social readjustment under the impulsion of the ideals of God in Christ.

Addressing "the slaves," Paul enjoins them voluntarily to yield the obedience demanded by the social pattern: "Give obedience to your lords on the human basis (the according to the flesh lords) with full respect and careful concern, in single hearted motive ('simplicity' means with no duplicity and no divided motive) as (giving obedience) to your (the) Christ" (5). They are to see the Christ in the human master, or else, if that cannot be, to look beyond the master and see the real Master. This spirit calls for some further definition, and Paul gives it with frank recognition of some of the most glaring sins and evasions of servants, whether slaves or employes, indeed, in all relations to others. They are to perform duties and tasks "not on the plane of eye-service as men-pleasers, but as servants of Christ occupied in doing the things that God desires with eagerness (out of the soul) (6), serving in all good will as to the Lord and not to men," so fully will you be aware of this primary relation to the Lord (7).

All the while you will be acting "in the knowledge ('knowing') that each man, whatever he may do that is good (there is no essential difference of meaning in the extensive variations of the Greek text here) will receive that in recompense from the Lord, whether slave or freeman" (8). We are in all things dealing with and working under the Lord, no matter how conditioned humanly.

(b) The same principle applies to masters, plus the added responsibility of their position (9a). To be in any position where one's will and disposition extends itself and finds enlarged expression in the directed will and actions of others is to come into expanded and deepened responsibility. The ethical burden of using the physical and the spiritual energies of other human beings for whatever cause is more than any human being should undertake except in the fear of God and with a definite sense of divine calling.

"You masters, too, do the same things toward them." Act on the same principles and in the same spirit in your dealing with the servants as have been prescribed for them, "abstaining from (all use of) the (method of) threatening." That is, deal with them on the basis of men on a common plane of friendliness and brotherly good will. This is emphasized by placing "the same things" before *"do."*

(c) Both alike are slaves of the Lord and subject to impartial judgment (9b). You are always to act "knowing that both their and your Lord is in heaven." Putting both genitive pronouns before the substantive, and the repetition of the *"and"* with "their" and "your," emphasizes that the same Lord is Lord of both. And the Lord of both slave and master is located in heaven, where all is as it should be, while he looks upon you on earth. "And (you will know) that with him there is no partiality" (9b). The order and idiom give significant emphasis, "and regard for superficial appearance (face) is not in his presence."

The Christian principles, ideals, and warnings of this condensed statement apply to all relations where men live and serve under men, whether as personal slaves, employed workmen, groups of laborers of all classes, under all kinds of economic or institutional forms or systems. Accepted and applied in good will and with intelligent co-operation these principles would solve all problems in the economic and business world. Paul here has in mind household adjustments, including the slave-master economy of his day. In the entire passage, from 5:21 to 6:9, he is exhorting to the attainment of the true Christian household. With the wider applications he is not here dealing, nor with the changes his principles would bring about in the social order. These are left for time and development.

VI

THE GLORIOUS WARFARE AND VICTORY OF THE CALLED—6:10-20

There is much more to say in unfolding the full meaning of the Body of Christ in expressing and applying "the gospel of the glory of the blessed God." It can never all be said. There are rigid limits on what Paul, under his imprisonment conditions, can write. He has defined the Church as God's creation through Christ Jesus and as such the channel of his achieving purpose in human and universal history. He has shown that the Christ requires the Church as his completing counterpart in incorporating his divine personality as redemptive and consummating agency of God's love for a sinful world. He has made clear the dependence of all the saints and the Church of the saints upon the Spirit of God uniting them and sanctifying them and empowering them for their function in society as its saving and enlightening factor through the course of history. He has set this Church down in the midst of an alien, depraved world, there to enlighten, reprove, and save the members of worldly society. He has enunciated the principles that are to control in the Christian community. Now "as for what is left" to say, he can only warn them of the nature of the struggle they are to have, list the resources and weapons with which their battles are to be won, and challenge to faithful, courageous, and victorious acceptance of the conflict with the forces of evil.

Always with a martial militancy of soul, and an aspiring spirit, Paul made much use of the vocabularies of athletics and the terminology of warfare. He is always quick to sense the enemies of the Christ and of "all who will live godly in Christ Jesus." He learned to appraise "the enemies of Christ" and of the Christian aim and ethic and to overcome them. He knew the systems of philosophy, theories of society, and institutions of religion that deceived men and ensnared their souls with subtleties. So he warned his fellow Christians and especially their leaders, of the dangers, in every epistle of his, from First Thessalonians to the last Pastoral, even as Jesus had done in his day, and as did John; even as Peter also was ready to remind his hearers of the qualities that mark the Christian way of life, and thought it right so long as he was in this tabernacle to continue keeping those who shared the faith in the righteousness of God awake to their call and to the dangers that beset it. (2 Pet. 1; especially 12-15ff; 2:18-22).

The manuscripts are too nearly balanced between "henceforth" (ablative, or genitive singular) and "as for the rest" (accusative plural) for us to be quite certain of the reading; nor does it make any great difference. Indeed the two idioms might mean the same thing. "As for the rest"—that is involved and invites discussing, seems to fit the connection better; "from now on" hardly seems to be called for. Thus is introduced

1. The call to spiritual war, 10-18.

Besides the general tendency of Paul's spirit, his close and continuous contact with Roman soldiers for four years now had stimulated his active mind in developing detailed comparisons between military activity and equipment and the Christian conflict and resources.

(1) First of all is the attitude and strength of the soldier of the Christ, as of the soldier of Caesar (10-11). "Be endued with strength in the Lord and in the (consciousness of) the grip of his strength" (10). You are in the Lord and in his service as he carries on his warfare against all that is evil. That consciousness arouses all your strength and courage. There is more: "You are in the grip of the supreme strength which the infinite Lord puts forth in his soldiers." One is reminded of Jehovah's preparation of Joshua to take up the conquests bequeathed to him by the death of Moses (Josh. 1:1-9). Similar assurances are given on many occasions in the course of "the battles of the Lord" in the Old Testament history. Nor can we

fail to think of Jesus' preparation of the Twelve for their conflicts, especially in John 16.

But even the empowered soul, full of the courage of well-grounded confidence, must make full preparation: "Put on the panoply of God" (11)—the complete armor with all the instruments provided for protection and aggression. It is God's equipment provided by him and required by him for use of his soldiers. All this is necessary, "looking to your being able to stand in the face of the schemes of the devil" (11). The devil, opponent of God and of his commander, Christ, plans and directs the forces of opposition. He has "his methods," his plan of campaign, his strategies, his tricks. He is never to be taken lightly, nor are the Christian soldiers ever to permit themselves to be taken off guard. Paul took Satan very seriously. So did Jesus. We would be foolish not to take him seriously. That is one of his most deceiving and successful "wiles," to lead men to take him lightly. In warfare, to anticipate the enemy's plans and to divine his schemes are marks of highest generalship, if at the same time the general is always making full use of his own resources.

(2) The terrific nature of the conflict is next stressed as a reason for the injunctions of verses 10-11 (12).

The passage has its difficulties. They are largely due to the condensed crowding of so much into few words, so characteristic of this Epistle. They also grow out of our lack of full knowledge of the thought climate of that period. The main purpose is obvious: to direct the minds and set the wills of Paul's readers to the spiritual and intellectual plane on which their warfare must be waged; to the desperate and determined campaign against them because of their relation to their Lord Christ; to the infinite importance of the issues at stake, their own deliverance, the honor of their Redeemer, the hope of humanity, the glory of God. He ignores all purely physical opposition, persecution, and hardships, to center all concern on winning the Christian victory over all enemies in the realm of heavenly relations and values.

"For the contest (set) for us is not against blood and flesh."

Here Paul uses not a word for battle, or even war, but the more general term which may include warfare and battles, along with all kinds of contests, even athletic competitions. Some of the translations seek to express it by *"we wrestle not."* "Us" is dative, signifying the contest with which we are concerned; and this concern is made the more emphatic by the strong negative coming first after *for.* Here is the order: "For not is for us the contest (one in which we are) facing blood and flesh." We might speculate on Paul's reason for "blood and flesh" rather than the usual "flesh and blood" (e.g., 1 Cor. 15:50). We should not change the order. In any case he is saying that our enemies are not merely human; they are demonic personalities conducting a warfare against the purposes and plans of God in Christ. Our human opponents are inspired and used by superhuman forces of evil which they represent, consciously or unconsciously.

We, on our part, must be consciously empowered and directed by the superhuman Spirit. We are fighting cosmic battles. Therefore we struggle not with merely human forces "but, on the contrary, against the organized systems of rule, against the organized realms of authority, against the integrated rulers of this Darkness, against the spiritual forces of wickedness in the heavenly relations." "The heavenly" is an adjectival phrase with no substantive specified. It is usually—mistakenly—completed as "heavenly places." The locale of the conflict here can hardly be in heavenly *places.* That hardly makes sense, notwithstanding extended explanations by learned expositors. It does not make good sense in other passages; e.g., 1:3, 20; 2:6; 3:10. Philippians 3:20 may be local in concept, but the whole range of Christian faith is in spiritual meanings and relations for which the physical location is only symbol and thought pattern. In every use in Ephesians we are in the superphysical realm of thought. Here it is the nature of our conflict and the character of our opposition that are before us, involving all heavenly interests.

The use of the article with plurals in connection with "rules," "authorities," "world-rulers," "spiritual (forces)," marks them as definite, systematized, organized. "World-rulers" is a compound word (κοσμοκράτωρας) literally meaning order-rulers which we have tried to express by "integrated rulers." It suggests "united in federation." The thought systems and vocabularies of Paul's day had these spiritual powers systematized in a way unfamiliar to modern thought and speech. We have gotten too far away from assurance of their reality. We have killed the devil in our philosophy and largely in our theology and banished all his hosts from our "scientific minds"; yet in all the realms of life he and they are still rampant and destructive. It is easier to expel the devil from theology than to bar him from even our churches, to say nothing of our social institutions and secular combinations.

(3) Items of our winning panoply, 13-17.

Because of the nature of our conflict and our enemies and of all the issues involved, "on this account take up the entire-armor of God," which his grace and prevision have provided (13a). The original basis of this figure is found in Isaiah 59:17, where God himself "puts on righteousness as a breastplate, and a helmet of salvation upon his head, and garments of vengeance, and clothes himself with zeal as a mantle"; and goes forth to overwhelm his enemies. Paul first employed the figure in 1 Thessalonians 5:8 where Christians are exhorted to put on "the breastplate of faith and love, and for a helmet the hope of salvation." Now he has developed the figure in detail with extended correspondences between the accouterments of the soldier and the equipment of the warring saint.

The Christian must omit none of the armor "in order that ye may be 'able to stand your ground' (Weymouth) in the evil day, and having fought the battle to a finish in all its phases (having wrought-through the whole gamut of conflicts) to stand," victors in complete possession of the field (13). "The evil day" might mean the time of special, determined efforts to destroy the Christian movement, of which Paul warns repeatedly as being imminent (2 Thess. 2:1-12; Acts 20:28-31; 1 Tim. 4:1-5, etc.). It is better to understand it as referring to any time when the great battle is pitched, as it is again and again. This general summary call to full preparation for complete victory is followed up now with details, as piece by piece the soldier gets himself fully armed. "Take your stand then" equipped, assured, and ready for the conflict. How we are to be thus ready is given now item by item (14-17).

"Having girded your loins with (the belt of) truth." No loose garments are to be left to hinder any movement in the task to which you are wholly committed. And the belt gives the feeling of compact strength and control of the body. The girdle for the spirit is "truth." The sense of the word here is integrity, consistent devotion of all one's powers, and their integration in undivided co-ordination. Ethical and moral consistency within the self and with the character and purpose of God is suggested. In Romans 15:8, Paul affirms that "the Christ became a ministering servant (διάκονος) of the circumcision (the Jewish people) in the interest of the truth of God," so that God's promises to the fathers should be confirmed; i.e., that the integrity of God should be maintained and recognized. Before any outward armor, one must have inner integrity and stability. Not all the outside armor can save the unstable soul.

"And having put on the breastplate of righteousness." Certainly Christian righteousness is God's gift. But it is a gift conferred by the only method by which character can be given, through achievement. God's righteousness for man is "by faith." It is first of all "imputed." It is also imparted. Both are "by faith" and "through faith," "from faith to faith" (Rom. 1:17; 3:30). We have our standing before God by reason of the righteousness of Christ Jesus. We stand before men by reason of his righteousness having produced righteousness in us. The vital parts of the body are protected by the breastplate, and while the soldier faces forward toward the enemy. Righteousness which cannot be impugned is an essential protection against slander, suspicion, vituperation.

"And having shod the feet with the readiness of the gospel of peace." The "and" singles out each item as it is mentioned. The armor is not put on all in one piece. It constitutes a unified protection, complete when every piece is individually adjusted in its proper place. There must be readiness, facility, skill for going anywhere, over all obstacles, with the gospel of the peace which God, through us, offers to all men in the blood of the Christ. That readiness for conflict and for spiritual conquest comes in the form of the "blessed assurance" of peace with God which the gospel has brought to the believer. He is strong in the sense of his at-one-ness with God.

We should not exclude, as some expositors do, the further sense of readiness to proclaim the gospel of peace. The Christian soldier's preparation is first of all peace between himself and God. This experience gives him a gospel even for God's enemies, who are his enemies only because God's enemies. God comes with the good news of peace for all, the distant and the near (2:17). Having received that peace as his very own, one is ready for the conflict, because he has the gospel of peace for all. The Christian soldier is not fighting these spiritual enemies merely for his own protection and salvation. He is fighting to rescue men from sin and rebellion in themselves and from the superhuman forces of sin. While he must be a determined, persistent fighter, he is also the messenger of peace, always calling out to human enemies "in behalf of the Christ: 'Be ye reconciled to God' " (2 Cor. 5:20).

The Christians' fighting is "offensive warfare." They must go. Therefore they must be shod with eager readiness for evangelism (15). Yet must we keep always in mind that as Christ's soldiers we are not fighting sinners but the sin sources back of these human sinners.

"Along with all (the rest) taking up the great-shield of faith with which (as they strike in it) you will be able to quench all the missiles of the wicked one, those that have been set burning" (16). It is a pregnant phrase. The large shield of the Roman soldier was large enough (4 x 2½ ft.) to protect the body. It would catch and stop all the darts and would quench those that had been dipped in pitch and set on fire. The Christian faith would nullify even the fiercest instruments of the enemy's attacks. An adequate faith is invincible and secure.

To this point the items have been introduced by participles, equipping the Christian soldiers to "stand" ready for battle.

Now a new imperative is introduced for two other items. "And take the helmet of salvation and the sword of the Spirit which is the word of God" (17). The verb in verse 13 is "take up." Here it is the simple form "take" and has the meaning "receive," which may be the reason for the syntactical change. The salvation and the Word of God are peculiarly, but not exclusively, the gift of the Spirit which one receives. This is not to be insisted on, however; the distinction cannot be too sharp. The helmet is the consciousness of salvation; in 1 Thessalonians (5:8) it is "the hope of salvation." Salvation is both a fact as the gift of God to faith, and a hope, as it is to be perfected in the future. It is in both passages the protection for the head.

Was Paul thinking of the wiles of the enemy aimed especially at the head, the pride of wisdom, the systems of philosophy; theosophical speculations; delusions of immoral ethical theories? His references to these are so numerous and so serious as to require no listing of them here. Colossians, written in close relation to this Epistle, deals with dangers and delusions of the early gnosticism and phases of docetism, asceticism, and Epicureanism. In 2 Corinthians 10:3-6 he deals briefly with the forces of rationalism and the strongholds of wordly wisdom which defy the knowledge of God. In words very similar to this passage, he says: "The weapons with which we fight are not human weapons, but mighty for God in overthrowing strong fortresses" (Weymouth). He goes on to say that all these he can overthrow and can bring into subjection for the obedience of the Christ every thought-construct (theory); that he holds himself ready for such victories whenever the Christians' obedience is complete.

"And (receive) the sword of the Spirit"—the sword which he forged and gives and in the use of which he instructs and for the wielding of which he gives the power. This sword "is the word of God." Its quality and capacity are most strikingly set forth in Hebrews 4:12-13. The word as a weapon of the Messiah was a figure of great force in Isaiah 11:4 in a connection in which other items of conquering instruments are named. "He will smite the earth with the rod of his mouth and with the breath of his lips slay the wicked." Again in 49:2 "his mouth is like a sharp sword." In the vision of the Christ in the midst of his churches in the Revelation, chapter 1, John saw "proceeding from his mouth a sharp two-edged sword," and the figure is used in subsequent chapters.

"The word of God" was not, of course, exactly our Bible, nor was it exactly the Hebrew Scriptures, although they do in a large way represent it. "The word of God" is his expressed will and purpose, however expressed; his principles and judgments. These the Christian warrior is to know and use. The Bible will be the first, most important, the only finally reliable Word of God, if under the guidance and illumination of the Holy Spirit it becomes the revelation of the Personal Word, Jesus Christ, the Son of the Father.

(4) Continuous prayerful watchfulness is enjoined in verse 18. Without that the warrior cannot use his perfect armor for successful fighting and glorious victory. Some commentators treat this as an item in the armor. It is better to treat it as the attitude and conscious experience of the soul through every stage of his battles and with each use of every weapon of defense and of offense. "By use of every approach and expression of prayer and petition, continuously praying (present tense) on every occasion in the Spirit, and watching out for it with full earnestness (application of strength) and with entreaty concerning all the saints." Salmond (Exp. Gk. Test.) admirably points out that praying is here "defined in respect of its *variety* and *earnestness*, its *constancy* and its *spiritual reality*."

"Watching out for *it*" is general, "it" having no specific antecedent. This produced some confusion for manuscript copyists and gives grammatical commentators trouble. Whatever the specific object of the prayer at any moment, and in the interest of the victory, in the whole contest the petitioners are to watch for their own use of each occasion and against every device of the enemy. The word "watching" means being alert, staying awake.

And we are to be comprehensive in our praying, "in behalf of all the saints." The cause is one, the fighters are all part of the army of the Lord. As Paul begins his discussion (1:15) with emphasis on the common faith and love among all the saints, and stresses the unity of all the called throughout the Epistle, so in this closing call to prayer in the midst of the conflict each one is to pray for all. No section of the Christian army and no single soldier can be at his best if he forgets the other sections and soldiers. There is an indispensable unity of the forces of Christianity demanded for its conflict. We forget that to our own danger, to the hindrance of the campaign, and at the price of disloyalty to the one "Captain of our salvation." Here is one most serious weakness in the Christian mission in the world.

2. God's Ambassador calls for special prayer in his own behalf. "And in behalf of me especially (emphatic form of the pronoun, (ἐμοῦ), 19-20.

Paul's pleas for prayer in his own behalf and his expressions of dependence upon this is a characteristic note in his writings. See 1 Thessalonians 5:25, "Brethren pray concerning us"; 2 Thessalonians 3:1-2, where one of two specific prayers requested is to the same effect as here; Philippians 1:19, "I know that this (imprisonment experience) will result in my salvation (in the sense of his ministry) through your supplication and the supply of the Spirit; 2 Corinthians 1:10-11, ". . . on whom we have set our hope that he will again deliver us, ye also adding your energies in our behalf in prayer," with the outcome that "many thanks may be given by many persons on our behalf." Most intense and full of all such pleas is that in Romans 15:30-32. Here, with a most solemn appeal, he asks the Roman saints to "toil together with" him in their prayer in his behalf, and proposes a list of specific objects for the praying. In connection with his earnest appeal for prayer in his behalf, we must remember his constant assurance of his prayer for his fellow Christians.

In our passage here, while Paul indicates but one object of prayer ("in order that," ἵνα), by his phrasing he breaks it into three items, all pointing to faithful and successful testimony in the gospel.

(1) The first, more general, prayer is to be "that to me may

be given utterance," which means spiritual freedom, "in opening my mouth." It is a prayer that the Spirit will give him definite sense of message and readiness of speech in expressing it in his delivery of the message in effective formulation.

(2) To this desire for inner freedom by reason of consciousness that God is speaking through him (cf. 3:12; 1 Cor. 2:13, a fuller expression of the whole idea), Paul would have them pray that he have full courage in the face of men, "in boldness to make known the mystery of the gospel, in behalf of which I am serving-as-ambassador in a chain." The limitation of the chain by which he was bound to a guarding soldier was symbol of all the hindrances and deterrents to discharging fully his duties as God's ambassador on behalf of Christ. (See 2 Cor. 5:20 and context where this ambassadorship is more fully stated, and the only other New Testament use, specifically, of this ambassador concept.) Paul has explained in 3:4-6 what this "mystery" (intimate ideal of God) is as now revealed in the gospel; and he has explained in 3:7-9 his own special appointment as the interpreter of this divine secret so that all men might know it, and that God may be glorified through the knowing.

The "chain," meaning all the restraints of four years in Roman prisons, might tend to discourage the ambassador and make him cautious, or even to induce him to seek his own release at the expense of full delivery of his gospel. So he keeps his responsibility and his high honor before him and seeks the support of intercession of his brethren that he may unhesitantly and faithfully speak his mesage to soldiers, officers, judges, and rulers. Quite probably he is thinking of what may be a determinative hearing of his case very soon and desires to use the occasion, as he did before Felix and before Festus and Agrippa.

(3) He comes, therefore, to the third term, which is a second specific defining of that for which he requests prayer, "that in it (this mystery of the gospel) I may be courageous (to declare it) as I ought to speak" (20). It is most impressive that Paul is so concerned about being courageous. We think of him as lacking

nothing in bravery. Perhaps his standards were higher than ours. If he needed so much prayer for courageous fidelity to his calling, what of us?

FINAL WORDS—6:21-24

1. Information about himself

Paul recognizes that in the first instance all who read his exposition of the Christian Calling or hear it read will be concerned to know his present status and all they may learn about his welfare and his work. They have all either become Christians under his direct and indirect missionary ministry or have known much of his wide and vast labors and influence.

Tychicus, who bears the letter, is one of his chief helpers. We first meet him as a member of the delegation Paul organized to accompany him when he took the relief funds to Jerusalem at the close of his third period of missionary travels (Acts 20:3ff.). With Trophimus he represented the churches of the province of Asia, of which there were already a number of representatives, one from each principal area. Whether he was of Ephesus, as Trophimus was (Acts 21:29), or of another city is not told. He seems to have been closely associated with Paul during much of his third mission period and to the end of his life, and to have been thoroughly devoted, trustworthy, and greatly beloved by the busy and aging apostle (Eph. 6:21; Col. 4:7; Titus 3:12; 2 Tim. 4:12). We may suppose that he made the round of all the Asia churches with the circular letter, reading it at each place, giving information concerning Paul and the whole situation at Rome, and conducting forums for exposition and inquiry. He accompanied Onesimus to Colossae with the letters to the Colossians and to Philemon. The more elaborate commendation of him in the Colossian Epistle (4:7-9) may indicate that Tychicus had some special association with the saints there.

"In order that you may know, you in your turn, my situation in full (the things pertaining to me), how I fare, all matters Tychicus will make known to you, my ('the') beloved brother and faithful minister (to me) in the Lord." If this was a circular letter, the greeting would come to each group in order, and so the addition "and" you (καὶ ὑμεῖς) is appropriate as indicating Paul's thought of each of the churches to which the Epistle was to be carried.

Tychicus is commended as "the beloved brother and faithful minister." The word is "deacon" (διάκονος), which never in the New Testament comes to be definitely a technical, official designation. Does any term become official and specific? The relation between Tychicus and Paul was, of course, "in the Lord," as were all relations, functions, and activities for Paul. In Colossians, as indicated above, Paul adds to his epithets here that Tychicus is his "fellow-slave." In both Epistles, in identical words, he says of him, "whom I (have) sent unto you, for this very purpose, that you may be informed about us and that he may encourage your hearts."

2. Benediction on all genuine lovers of Jesus Christ (23-24)

Now the final word of prayer for the saints, and blessing upon them. "Peace to the brethren (a name that derives from Jesus himself and much used by the early Christians) and love with faith, from God (the) Father and (the) Lord Jesus Christ." The omission of the article with Father and with Lord may be significant. All three qualities, peace, love, faith, to be continued and enriched by the joint giving of Father and Lord, always one in relation to men. Faith, in Paul's thinking, is the basic bond by which men are originally and continuously bound to God. But faith must not be narrowly conceived. It is vitalized and activated by love and it works in the bouyant consciousness of peace with God.

"God's (the) grace (be) with all who are lovers of our Lord ('the Lord of us') Jesus Christ in uncorruptibility." The continuing grace of God sustains continuing security, faithfulness, growth, and service for all in whom that grace evokes their incorrupt love for Jesus as the Christ of God and the Lord. Fitting close to Paul's deepest and most complete word about "the high calling of God in Christ Jesus."

Paraphrase

It is never possible to speak or write all that is in one's mind. Speech is never in a vacuum. It has a context and an atmosphere. These are a vital part of what one is saying and must be sensed and measurably felt if the hearer or reader is to understand, get the intent and content of the communication. For that reason, and all the more, no translation of a writing in one language into another can ever be literal or complete. Hence the value of paraphrastic renderings of the Scriptures. Any intelligent reader more or less consciously constructs a paraphrase as he reads. Otherwise he gets a very limited and bare message. It is obviously important that the paraphrase reconstruct the thought context and the emotional states of the writer.

In the following paraphrase of Ephesians the obligations of fidelity to Paul have been accepted in prayerful seriousness. Account has been taken of all one knows and feels of the apostle's background, history, personality, and experiences. On all these Paul drew in writing this extraordinarily condensed summary of all he had known and felt concerning Jesus Christ as Revealer of God, Saviour of men, Founder of his Church, Lord of life and of history, continuous Presence through the Spirit in the progress of the gospel. Here are his experiences, his beliefs and his creed, his hopes and his assurance. Here is what God has revealed to him and commissioned him to say to the Church and through the Church to the world from age to age concerning the divine intention in history unto its consummation.

An honest, reverent effort is here made to reproduce the context in Paul's own mind of the words which he was writing down in these few condensed pages. Not all that Paul was thinking can be put into a paraphrase, of course. The circle of his thought was vast. Only what would seem to be the immediate context in thought of what he was putting to parchment is undertaken. For the most part, modern applications have been avoided, great as was the temptation, except by suggestion and by implication in the forms of statement. At some points a bit of elaboration was found necessary to correct what the paraphraser was deeply convinced are vital misconceptions of the thought and intent of the original writing.

It hardly needs to be said that a paraphrase must break up the sentences of the writer. That is especially true of Paul, some of whose sentences run into a dozen lines and require closest attention to hold their parts in relation and balance. In the paraphrase, words that represent translation are *italicized.* The reader will see that these words, when all the other words are omitted, will yield a continuous version of the original writing. For this rendering, as for that which will follow in simple form without paraphrase, the author assumes responsibility. He has consulted many English versions but has followed none in his effort to translate the Greek of the Epistle.

PARAPHRASE

CHAPTER I

1 *Paul, representative of Christ Jesus,* called and *sent*
through a specific choice of *the will of God,* addressing himself
to the set apart and committed *people of Christ who are* (in
Ephesus, and any other city to which the Epistle comes) and
who in their situation are *faithful in* their relation to *Christ*
2 *Jesus* and in the realm of his purpose for them. I wish for you
grace and peace which come *to you from God* who relates
himself to us as *our Father and* who acts through and in unity
with him whom we have accepted as our *Lord, Jesus Christ.*
3 *Blessed,* with our worthy recognition and praise, *be the God*
who is *also Father of him* who is *our Lord,* the human *Jesus,*
the divine *Christ.* He is to be blessed by us because it is *he*
who himself beneficently *blessed us in every* kind of *blessing*
that has to do with our *spiritual* welfare in the realm of *our*
heavenly relationships, blessings which are all comprehended
4 in God's dealing with us *in Christ.*
This comprehensive blessing which we receive relates us
definitely to the continuous development of God's purpose and
plan in Christ, *even as he chose us in him,* in whom God ever
deals with men, *before* his *projection of the world order.* In
this choice God was *looking to our being separated* from all
evil and diverting courses and connections so as to be *also*
blameless in character and conduct, as we live and function
5 *in his full view.* Confirming and carrying out this choice
and plan, *in* his *love* he *marked us off before* the beginning
of human history *with a view to our being set into sonship*
unto himself by means of the work and influence of *Jesus*
Christ.
All this plan of God for us and his dealing with us was
grounded in and is carried out fundamentally only *in accord-*
6 *ance with the good pleasure of his active will;* and is *intended*
to issue in praise of the glory of his grace through universal
recognition of that grace as it is made evident *in his being*
gracious to us, when we were wholly without claim on his
7 favor, by his choosing and claiming us *in his Beloved* Son; *in*
whom we have in actual experience *our ransom through his*
sacrificial *blood* in our behalf. This ransom includes *the bear-*
ing away of our defections, wherein we fell outside the path
of his ideal for us.

8 This gracious ransom and forgiveness and induction into
sonship are without limit since they are *in accord with the*
richness of his grace which he caused to come into us in over-
flowing stream, resulting *in every form of wise insight-*
9 *discernment,* by means of which he *caused us to know the*
essential inner content of that which he had determined upon
in the Christ. All this is *according to a plan* and method
originating in *his good pleasure* and *which he projected in*
10 *him, in order to* set up through us who are thus incorporated
with the Christ *a stewardship* of history *for realizing the full*
plan of God by making use *of the opportunities* provided in
the course of history; and so to bring about the goal of all
history making *in the heading up of all things in orderly* and
harmonious completion *in his Christ, the things in the heavens*
above and the things upon the earth. For all that exists is to
be perfected into one order even as all things exist in the unity
11 of the purpose of God's grace.
All we who are his are thus incorporated with the Christ
of God and find our meaning in relation to him, because God
creates and carries on history *in him, in whom also we were*
made God's *heritage, which* was indicated by our *having been*
so designated by God's *marking us off as his in accordance*
with his plan, who is accomplishing all things in accordance
with the deliberate plan, which always characterizes *his will.*
12 It was thus planned *that we who have previously cherished*
hope in the promised and achieving *Christ might be* instrumental *unto the praise of his glory* by what we did and represented by our testimony and course in history.
13 Yet we who have previously cherished the hope of the
promised Christ have no exclusive or peculiar claim to him.
God's heart and plan are comprehensive in Christ, *in whom*
you also, of the non-Jewish races as well as we Jews, *having*
heard the divine *message of the true mind* of God, as it came
to you in *the good news of your salvation* provided in Christ,
and having put your trust in him, received upon you *the seal*
of the Spirit whom Christ *promised* to them that accept him,
the Holy Spirit who manifested himself in supernatural and
superhuman demonstration. It is the Spirit *who is,* by this
14 stamp of his ownership, a *pledge of our* belonging to God, *his*
heritage, thus identified as his while as yet we are incomplete,
until the full redemption of that upon which God is ever
working.

This outcome of complete possession of his redeemed, just as we have seen in the plan of God, and in the atonement

of the beloved Christ, so now in the sealing and achieving
work of the Holy Spirit, is for, and will be effective in, *"the
praise of his glory."*

15 *Because of this plan of God in Christ Jesus,* to be realized
through the Holy Spirit, *because of* this purpose of his grace
and the glory which is to come to him in the working out of
redemption in human history, and *because of* the experience
of grace working already in those who have heard and accepted this good news, *I also,* linking myself up with the triune
God, join with you in rejoicing over your inclusion in this
experience, and so *having heard* about *the faith in the Lord
Jesus that obtains among* you, *and* about *the love which you*
16 *cherish toward all the Lord's people, I do not cease in my*
17 *rejoicing over you, making specific mention of you on* the
occasions of my praying.

My grateful prayer is *to the God of* him who by his grace
is now *our Lord Jesus Christ,* the God who is *the Father of
Glory,* himself all-glorious and the source and center of all
that is glorious. To him my prayer is *that he will give to you*
through the inworking of his Spirit, *a spirit of insight and of*
18 *revelation* resulting *in* the *accurate knowledge of him,* and so
knowledge of the deeper meanings of truth and reality, a spirit
which he will give by *the eyes of your heart having been
enlightened,* since the source and issues of living knowledge
are found in the basal heart attitudes.

The objective in my prayers for this insight on your part
into God and into his purpose in his people is, *that you may
know* in experience: first, *what is* God's optimistic aim in
calling men into his redemption and fellowship, *the hope
of his calling;* second, *what* is the *wealth of the glory* which
God expects to acquire as he comes into possession *of his*
19 *inheritance in his saints* whom he redeems through his Beloved
Son and sanctifies by his Spirit; third, *what is the more-than-
sufficient greatness of his dynamic power which he brings
into operation in us who continuously trust him,* in order that
he may realize his wealth and fulfill his hope in our calling.
This power is the same as and is *in accord with the energy of*
20 *the active-grappling* with our problem of even *his* infinite
*strength which he put-forth-energetically in the Christ when
he raised him out from among dead bodies.*

And, not only did he raise the Christ from the dead but,
when he had set him on his right hand in the heavenly realms,
21 whence the cosmic worlds are controlled and human history,
there he was placed *clear above,* superior to and authoritatively

over, *every form and order of rule and authority and power and lordship, and every name that is named not only in this present age but also in the age that is to come.* All was placed under his rule and plan. Thus God fulfilled the declaration
22 of the ancient Scriptures and the word of Jesus in his assurance to his apostles, for he *also put* the ordering of *all things under his feet.*

And, with all this authority in heaven and on earth now established in the exalted Christ, God *gave him* the function
23 and relation of exclusive *Head over all things to the Church,* the Church *which,* in its turn in the appointment of God and in the plan of human history in relation to cosmic history, *is his Body,* without which the Christ is incomplete as God's cosmic Authority. As the Body of the Christ functioning in human history, the Church is *the full expression and historic content of* the Christ who is, as thus completed in his Church Body, *the one who is fulfilling all things in all respects* in the progress and realization of God's purpose. The Christ is the full expression of God, and the Church the full expression and fulfilment of the Christ.

CHAPTER II

1 *And* God who raised and exalted the Christ comes to *you*
2 as *being* spiritually *dead-bodies* and destined for eternal death *by reason of your failures and your sins, in which it was formerly your habit to conduct your lives in accordance with* the spirit and practice of *the age of this world* in its unregenerate state, even *in accord with him who administers the corrupt authority which dominates the* demon filled *atmosphere, the spirit which* even *now is exerting himself effectively in the* motives, conduct, and society of the unbelieving world whose standards and conduct mark them as *children of dis-*
3 *obedience.* Yes, it was even such children of disobedience that *we all* were by nature when *among them* in our common sinful humanity *we lived our lives at one time in* the sphere of *the desire of our unregenerate human nature, being in the habit of doing the things determined by the unspiritual human nature and by our own private notions; and,* thus we *were in* our own *nature* properly to be regarded as *children of wrath even as* are *the rest* of men, not as yet come under the experience of God's grace.
4 *But,* instead of dealing with us as properly deserving wrath,
5 because of his *being rich in mercy* and *because of his great love*

with which he loved us even while we were, by reason of *our*
transgressions of the standards of righteousness, spiritually
dead-bodies, God, in purpose and in projected energy, *made*
us alive along with the Christ when he made him alive in the
tomb after his death on the cross. We must keep before us
6 the fact that *by grace you* have *been brought into the saved*
state. Yes, when he was raising the Christ from among the
physically dead bodies, putatively and in the intention of his
love God *raised us up* spiritually *along with* him; *and* he *set*
us down along with him in the heavenly realms and relations
as he incorporates us *in Christ Jesus,* thus uniting us with his
7 Christ in one unitary group.

By thus dealing with us God was *intending* and would be
able to have, *in* all *the succeeding ages, a* concrete *standing*
demonstration of the overflowing wealth of his gracious nature
in the fact of his *being* thus savingly *gracious in Christ Jesus*
to us who deserved only wrath.

8 *For it is by grace that you are in the state and relation of*
having been saved by nothing on your part but accepting
faith: and this experience of faith salvation is in *no* way de-
9 rived *from yourselves, God's gift* it is to you. It is *not* based
upon or produced *from works, so that no individual may*
10 *boast* of his righteousness, achievement, or character; *for* in
this matter of salvation *we are a product* of the will and working of *God,* having been *created by him* in his activity *in*
Christ Jesus with the intention of putting us *at* the task and
privilege of doing *good works, which God had prepared in*
anticipation of his spiritual creation of us *in order that* they
should constitute the sphere of our activity *as* God's people,
so that *we* are to *occupy-ourselves in* doing *them.* Thus are
we to fulfill God's creative purpose in our salvation.

11 In the light of this marvelous plan of God's grace and of
your experience of his gift of salvation, and in the light of
the relation of God's saved people to the Christ in whom God
is conducting the drama of human history, *do you therefore*
keep-constantly-in-mind the facts and the setting of your
salvation, *that you (the) Gentiles,* as the races have been
classified *on the flesh basis,* were men *called uncircumcisism*
by that which proudly *calls-itself the circumcision,* claiming
thus a religious sanction for racial exclusiveness and exaltation, although the distinction is quite superficial *only,* so to
12 speak, *handmade and limited to the flesh.* Still you are to
keep in mind that *at that time,* before your knowledge of

your being included in God's saving purpose, *you were out-*
side the Christ expectation and consciousness, in a condition
of *aliens from* the standpoint of *the commonwealth of Israel*
and strangers from the standpoint of *the covenants of* Messianic *promise,* which God had made with the Hebrews, having no recognized or conscious part in these, and so *not*
cherishing any hope and being people *without God in the*
cosmic and historical *order.*
13 *But now,* by glorious contrast, in the revelation of God's
comprehensive purpose and love and in your experience of
having been brought within the grace and power of Christ
Jesus, *you who were formerly in the condition of being far*
14 *away* from the God of peace *have come to be near in the blood*
of the Christ. For, when understood in his true character
and relation to mankind, *he* (the Christ), as God's redeeming
love manifest in human life, *is himself our peace,* ours without
distinction, for just as in Isaiah (57:19) God's Messenger is
heard proclaiming, "Peace, peace, to him that is far off, and
to him that is near, saith Jehovah, and I will heal him," so
in fulfilment in experience, the Christ is our peace, because
it is he *who* potentially and in purpose *made both* the divisions, Jew and Gentile, *one by destroying the* dividing *wall*
that made fragments of what was one in God's ideal, that wall
of racial and religious *enmity.*
This wall of separation Jesus utterly refused to recognize
and, because he was unrestricted in his human love and inter-
15 est, he *broke it down in his flesh, making noneffective* any
longer *the law of* the formal *commandments* expressed in
authoritatian decrees, because he grounded all relations in
reality and based religion on principle and the experience of
God. This he did *as a means by which he might create out of the*
two separated and antagonistic groups *one new human race,*
16 *effecting peace; and* in this peace-making process it was his
purpose that he *might harmonize both* the factional, fractional
divisions, *in one* unitary *body, reconciled to God through the*
mediating work and influence of *his cross, having by it utterly*
slain the enmity that broke men apart into antagonistic groups.
17 *And* so, *having come* on such a mission and with such a
basis of appeal in the atonement of his cross, *he began the*
proclamation of the good news of peace, to you, the ones
18 described by the prophets as *far away* from God *and peace to*
the ones who were regarded as *near.* Such is our good news
from God through his Christ, *because through him we have*

our common *approach, both of us, in one Spirit, unto the* one common *Father.*
19 *Well then,* in the light of all this, *you are therefore no longer* to be thought of by yourselves or by Jews at all as *strangers and* mere *visitors* in the realm of the redeeming God, *but* you are, in your own new right in Christ, *fellow-citizens among the people* of God's *Christ* and, in a more intimate and precious way of thinking, *members-of-the-family of God.*
20 Yes, again changing the form of stating what God's grace
does in us, you are to think of yourselves, in each race group,
as *a structure built upon the* eternal *foundation* of God's
purposes as announced in the messages and work *of the*
21 *apostles and prophets* of the gospel order, *Christ Jesus himself*
being the chief cornerstone in the entire structure which God
is building in human history. This structure of a redeemed
22 humanity is a vast, complex but unitary structure *in*
which every distinct building, as one race group after another is redeemed, *being harmoniously worked in with the rest* into the comprehensive architectural plan of the Great Builder, *makes a growing* addition *toward a temple sanctified* in the Lord unto God's glory, thus a temple *into which you, in your part, are in the precess of being constructed.* The great objective is *to provide a place of habitation for God,* who *in* his *Spirit* dwells in this new humanity.

CHAPTER III

1 *For the sake of this* structure of a holy temple of redeemed
humanity which God in Christ Jesus is building out of all
races, *I, Paul, the* man who has been made *a prisoner of the*
Christ, Jesus, because of my insistence on the inclusion of all
men without distinction in God's purpose of redemption, and
so Christ's prisoner *in behalf of you the Gentiles,* whom the
Jewish believers were not willing to accept freely in the
2 gospel—*if, indeed, as surely, you heard* with understanding
the stewardship of God's universal *grace* toward all men,
which was given to me with reference to you, the stewardship
which placed on me the high privilege and compelling obligation of getting God's grace on to you and to all the races,
3 you will know *how even on the basis of revelation was made*
known to me the inner content of God's purpose, *just as I*
4 *have briefly expressed it already.* And if you *consider* what
I have written *you will be able, by reading it carefully, to*

perceive my gift of *comprehension in* the matter of *the divine*
meaning of the Christ, which enables me to understand and
authorizes me to define God's idea and intent in his Christ,
5 you will see the deep meaning of God's way *which to other,*
preceding, *generations was not made known to the sons of*
men as it has now been disclosed by God as he makes himself
known *in the Spirit* by revealing it *to* his chosen and responsive
spokesmen and interpreters, *his holy apostles and prophets,*
under whose leadership he has entered upon the course of
making his grace universal by means of the gospel.
6 Here, then, is the great open secret which God wishes all
men to hear and understand: *That the Gentile peoples are,*
as truly as the Hebrews and along with them and on the same
terms, *a joint heritage* of God; that they constitute, along with
the Jews, all together, *a unitary corporate body; and* are *joint-*
participants in all *the promise* of God's purpose and redemption. All this is included in his plan *in Christ Jesus* and is to
7 be made actual *by means of the gospel, of which* in its marvelous comprehension and glorious content, *I got to be a minister*
on the score of the self-initiated grace of God which was
imparted to me by and on the scale of the active energy of
his power.
8 Yes, *even to me, who am less-than-least of all God's people*
consecrated in Christ, *was this grace given.* This grace of God
in me has two amazing and overwhelming aspects: (1) In my
own person as missionary, the *bringing to the heathen peoples*
the good news of *the wealth beyond all defining* which God
provides for all men in the person and work of *the Christ;*
9 *and* (2) the *bringing full light upon* what is God's method of
realizing his purpose, by *the stewardship of the* now revealed
secret of his purpose and plan in history *which has been con-*
cealed from the beginning through all *preceding ages in the*
God who created all things and who, therefore, rightly determines their course and determines the times and methods
10 of revealing his plans. This plan and method God adopted
and carried out *in order that now through* the presence and
faithful functioning of *the Church,* which he is creating and in
which his grace is manifested, *the many-sided wisdom of*
God may be made known to the ordered systems of rule and
authority in the heavenly realms. For indeed the history
of our race on earth may well appear as a contradiction of
God's wisdom and a denial of his righteousness, until it is
interpreted in the achievement of redemption by the Christ
through his Church.

11 All this plan of God, and its revealing and its working
out through the gospel and in the Church is now to be seen
to be not arbitrary or capricious but *according to a plan of*
constructing and directing *the ages,* which God *projected*
in Christ Jesus our Lord, through whom are all God's ap-
12 proaches to man and all his dealings with man, and *in whom,*
because we thus see his relation to the eternal God and to his
purposes in history, *we have our courage* to proclaim him
to any people under all conditions, *and* through whom we make
our approach to all men and gain *access, in* the *confidence*
inspired *by the faith* which makes us conscious instruments and
agents *of him.*

13 *Wherefore,* seeing that I am so related to God's cosmic purpose and to his redeeming Christ carrying on his plan of human history, *I beg you not to be unhappy in* the thought of *my afflictions in behalf of you,* for *even this* experience *is your glory,* inasmuch as you would not get the knowledge and benefit of the sacrifice of God's saving Son but by the afflictions of his servant who is bound to be identified with him in suffering for you.

14 Now to come to the prayer which I was about to make when
I paused to prepare you to understand and share its terms:
On account of God's plan in Christ Jesus and of my relation to
it all, *for this cause I bow upon my knees* in prayer *before the*
archetypal and supreme *Father, from whom,* in his attitude
15 and interest in all personal life, *every family* grouping of persons in social units both *in heaven and upon earth derives its*
name, as indicating its true nature and right ideal. Thus, I
now come to pray in behalf of you as members of that Church
which represents God in human history, and interprets him to
the intelligent cosmic world.

16 My prayer for you is *that* the Father *will give to you ac-*
cording to the spirit and measure of *the* infinite *wealth of his*
supreme *glory* the capacity and the experience of *being made*
so *mightily strong by his Spirit coming into* your *essential*
17 *being and* working *within you that the Christ* who is accomplishing God's program in history *may have his home in your*
hearts through your comprehending *faith* which will be such
as to accept him in his universal meaning and in his living
18 relation to all men. *With you* thus *thoroughly rooted and*
firmly founded in the principle and experience of *love,* the
basal factor and quality in God and in his course with men, so
that love will become the controlling emotion and motive in
your attitudes and behavior, I can now go on to pray *that you*

may be fully able, in conscious relation and fellowship *with*
all the people of God in Christ, to grasp fully what is the race-
wide *breadth* and *the* age-long *length* and *the* perfection *height*
19 and *the depth* beyond all our need, *yea even to know* in all its
dimensions *the love of the Christ,* his love for the world and
God's love of which he is the embodiment and the perfect expression. We must do our utmost to know that love *which*
in its full reaches *is beyond knowing.*

And so the object of my prayer is *that you may be filled*
with comprehension, with consecration and with the divine
achievement in you, all the redeemed together, *up to* the goal
at which God is aiming in his Christ and in his people, when
together they will include in corporate outcome *all the ful-*
ness of God in his redeeming plan and history-making work
in our human race.

20 *Now to him who has beyond all things* that may be involved
in it *power to do overwhelmingly more than* what *we are asking*
or even are capable of *thinking,* and able to do this *on the basis*
of the power which is continuously at work in us, to him be the
glory in the Church and in Christ Jesus, who together constitute the living unity of God in human history; glory to him
in Church and Christ, perfected in unity, *on into all the gen-*
erations of the age which is to be the consummation *of the*
ages. Amen.

CHAPTER IV

1 *Therefore,* seeing into how great a calling we are drawn
by God's grace, in being made sharers in his plan of the ages
and united with his Christ in fulfilling his glory under the
eager watching of the entire universe, *I, the* man *bound in*
prison because of my relation and my faithfulness *in the Lord,*
call you along to order your life in a way worthy of the calling
with which ye were called, worthy of the source, the sub-
stance, and the end of your high calling of God in Christ Jesus;
a calling which, as we have seen, places you in essential relation to God's purpose and plan, not only in history but even
also in God's cosmic creation.

2 The spirit of such worthy ordering of life and action will
be that *of unfailing humility* in *every* relation and experience
and of constant *meekness,* as those whom God's grace has so
marvelously honored. It will be a way of living set *in the*
very *midst of unflagging spiritual endurance,* manifest in *mu-*
tual and enduring support of one another in love, conscious that
the love of God has linked you all in interdependent relations

3 as an agency in his work. In this worthy response to your
marvelous calling, you will be *constantly eager to guard the unity of* spirit within the body of the called, conscious that thus maintaining and using this harmonious oneness for the divine ends is the function of *the Spirit,* and is thus a unity that must be jealously and zealously guarded and is kept unbroken because it is ever held *within the* unifying *bond of peace.*

4 Surely the functioning Body of the Christ in so great a
calling must live and work as one. See, then, the powerful appeal of a sevenfold unity in the very foundational and essential ideals and experiences of those who are within this calling: *One Body* of regenerated, uplifted sharers in God's plan; *and,* all together as well as individually, actuated by *One Spirit,* who is the life breath of the One Body; *according exactly* and necessarily with the experience wherein *you were* all *called in* the *One Hope of* God in *his calling you;* so that
5 we must all recognize in all things *One Lord,* into relations
with whom we have all alike come in the *One Faith* experience by which alone we share this calling; and we all signalized and sealed our union with the One Lord in the One Faith by the *One Baptism,* which for all of us was the putting on of the
6 Lord Jesus Christ; *One God* who is *also Father of All* the re-
deemed in Christ, members of this Church Body of Christ. And this one Father God sustains to all aspects, phases, and meanings of the entire cosmic and historic process, the threefold relationship of the One *who is over all and through all and in all* that is, and he is particularly over all and through all and in all the work of redemption and glory.

7 In this One Body whose unity must thus be insisted on and
jealously guarded, every individual has his own integral value, place, responsibility, opportunity, duty, *for to each one of us* members of the Unitary Body *singly* was *the grace,* allotted to him and designed to operate through him, *given in accordance with the measure of the free gift of the Christ,* who in the wisdom of his own plan and for his own work imparts the grace which enables each one of his own to take his place and fulfil his function in and in behalf of the whole.

8 *Wherefore,* in correspondence to this fact that the living
Christ distributes his grace by sovereign love to each of all his followers and thus makes them fit to be his gifts for service to men, we have the expression which *says* (Psalm 68:18):

> "Going up on high he led captive a band
> of captives,
> He gave gifts to mankind."

9 *Now the* idea in the phrase, *"He went up," what* else *does it*
involve if not that he also came down into the lower parts,
10 even into the realm of *the earth? The one who came down, in*
the incarnation and all its experiences and implications, *he is also the one who went up,* in ascension power and purpose, *on beyond all the heavens, in order that* as Master of earth and heaven *he might bring all things* in God's redemptive purpose *to* the *fulness* of glorious completion.
11 *And* thus the men whom he had captured by his redemption *he himself gave* to mankind through his Church, in which and for which they function, *some* of them to serve as *apostles,* who carry the Good News to new regions and groups of men; *some* as *prophets,* to interpret the presence of God in events attending the gospel and God's intention in the events; *some* to be *evangelists,* working from the bases established by the missionary apostles, and carrying the Good News to all the towns and villages in the region of these apostolic centers; *some* whose function is to be *pastors* and *teachers,* for the continuous training and care of those who are won by missionary work and evangelism.
12 The objective which the ascended Lord in all these creative functions in his Church is *facing* is *the perfecting of the saints in related unity for and in the work of service,* with *the* great
end in view of *the building up of the Body of the Christ.*
13 The standard and measure of this work on the part of the consecrated members of Christ's Body cannot be completed and perfected *until we all together achieve the goal* of *the unity* so essentially characteristic of the true Body of the Christ, the unity which is marked by and accomplished in the process *of the faith* which unites us *with God's Son, and* in such *accurate knowledge of him* as enables us to combine and cooperate with one another and with him in working out his purpose. This purpose is nothing short of our attaining *unto mature manhood,* yes even *unto the measure of the stature of the fully developed Christ,* who is growing his Body in the course of his redeeming work in human history, and who will not be the full-grown Christ until all his redeemed are perfected in unity.
14 This giving ourselves unitedly and co-operatively to the perfecting of the growing Body of the Christ involves *that we shall no longer be* content to remain *babes,* lacking in responsibility, understanding, and intelligent self-direction toward our goal, mere *tossing waves and carried around* here and there without aim or order *by every* chance *wind of teaching,* our

position and ideas being determined *by the* mere *dice-throw* of *those who are* only *men,* and by whom we would be led on
15 in *craftiness toward the deceit* which subtly betrays into the ways of *error. No,* the ideal and challenge of our relationship is, that *being true* in this relation to Christ and his calling, *in love* to him and to his people, and in devotion to his purpose, *we shall be ever growing,* in *all ways* and *all respects into* full relation and co-ordination with *him who is the Head* of this
16 Body which all we who are his do constitute, into *Christ, out of whom* as its source, its sustainer, its reason for existence and its hope and end, *all* parts of the *Body,* through *being harmoniously joined up together and being firmly knit together by means of every contact* by which *the supply* of growing grace from the Head flows *according to the active functioning in* its own proper *degree of each several part, produce the continuous growth of the Body, resulting in* its *building itself up,* the entire process being carried on by the constraint and inspiration of and *in* the atmosphere of *love.*

17 In view of God's calling of his saints in Christ Jesus, of our experience of his grace unto redemption, and of our relation to the Christ of history, as members of his Church Body through which he works and in which he finds his growing expression and his hope of perfection as Redeemer, we must recognize that there is a characteristic type of Christian living, personal and social, in the Church group, which must manifest itself in the social organism of the world and must be differentiated from all sinful and degenerate ways and works of men. Called into a new type of humanity, Christians must live as members of this new human race. *This, therefore, I declare* as the Christian ideal and calling, *and bear my testimony in the Lord,* as his servant and his commissioned interpreter: that as Christ's men and women, *you are to conduct your lives no longer* by the standards and behavior and *in accord with the way the pagan peoples conduct their lives, in the insane folly of their* unregenerate, purely human way of *think-*
18 *ing, being,* as they are, *darkened in* their *mental operations* and so unable to discern the meaning of life or the ways of rational living, because they *have alienated themselves from the life* which is characteristic *of God,* that life which he imparts to men and by which he would have men live. This secular, heathen way of looking at life is a condition which men have brought themselves into *by reason of the lack of understanding which,* in its turn, exists dominantly *within them because of the hardening of their heart* against the will and the gracious

19 goodness of God. Men thus disclose themselves as of *such*
depraved nature *as* that, *having come to be without moral*
sensitiveness or *sense of* shame, they have *delivered themselves*
over to complete indecency, committing themselves *to active*
indulgence in every form of uncleanness with insatiable desire.
20 *But ye did not thus learn the Christ,* that being in him, in
his Church, and joined with him in relation to God and God's
purpose in the world could leave us free for any measure of
21 fleshly indulgence or sharing in pagan social conduct, not,
indeed if it was *he whom ye heard and* if it was *in him* that
ye were instructed as to the meaning, the standards, the behavior of Christian living, that is if ye were taught *in true ac-*
cordance with truth concerning character and conduct as it has
been exemplified *in the* life of *Jesus* as he lived it on the human
plane and in relation to human society. What ye learned
22 in getting to know him was that as Christians *ye are to put off*
as filthy and repulsive garments *the old* unregenerate *humanity*
that was *characteristic of your former way of conducting your-*
selves, that old human nature *that is in process of corruption*
which goes on inevitably in a life that is conducted *according*
to the natural tendencies that inhere in *the deceit* of our sin-
23 ful nature. This true teaching as to the nature and method of
Jesus which we are to adopt as our own way of living is,
further, and positively, that ye are *to be made new,* on a higher
plane, *in the spirit of your mind,* that attitude and disposition which determine the approach to all conduct and the
24 ways of our behavior. *And* in this true learning of the Christ
you were instructed that as new creatures *ye are to clothe*
yourselves in the conduct that characterizes *the new human-*
ity which, according to the nature, standards, and purposes of
God was created by him, in his grace as he acted *in* the sphere
and interest of *righteousness and holiness,* which must be the
essential qualities and demands *of the truth* of reality in God.
25 *Wherefore,* as carrying out this "putting off" and "putting
on" of ways of conduct in the renewed life, *putting away defi-*
nitely what is false, do you all *individually speak truth* in all
relations *each one with his neighbor,* as God enjoined of old
(Zech. 8:16). This is the only intelligent and consistent way to
deal with our fellows, *for we are members of one another* in the
same body, where falseness is rightly unthinkable.
26 *Get angry,* as men will in impulsive reaction to irritating
surprises, *and* still *do not commit sin.* Maintain such control
and restraint, and effect so quickly the Christian adjustment
27 that you will *not permit the sun* of one day *to set upon your*

passing anger, nor, by cherishing a grudge, *give standing*
room in your life *to the devil,* who would thereby corrupt and
disrupt the Body. For the devil can work harm only as he
28 finds place in some life to do his evil work. *The one who has*
a habit of stealing, no longer let him steal, but rather let him
adopt the high Christian social ideals of manly independence
and brotherly helpfulness and *become a toiler, working at some*
good task with his own hands, no longer subsisting by the
labor of others, *in order that he may have,* as the product of
his toil, something *to share with* the *one who has* some worthy
actual *need.*

29 *Every word* which may occur to your mind but is *corrupt*
check and *let it not escape out of your mouth* to contaminate
the thought of others, *but if there is* in your thought *any good*
word that might tend *toward upbuilding* where *the need* for
constructive help exists, speak it out *in order to give grace to*
those that hear you. *And do not,* by anger or foul speech
or in any way, *grieve the Spirit who is holy,* the Spirit *of your*
God, the Spirit *in whom,* by his work in you making you children of God, *ye were sealed* with God's stamp marking you as
destined *unto a day of* his complete *redemption* of you.

31 *Every form of irritability, and quick temper, and wrath, and*
railing, and reviling, for these are all of a piece and one of
them leads on to the rest, *let* every one of them *be put away*
from you along with every kind of maliciousness, even in
thought, toward one another.

32 *Make yourselves graciously useful in* your relations *to one*
another, being well disposed, being gracious to one another, in
the spirit and *after the manner* of the true *God who was also*
on his part *gracious to us in Christ,* through whom God has
expressed himself toward man and who imparts to us as we
come into relations with him through Christ his own spirit
toward others.

CHAPTER V

1 *Make yourselves, therefore,* genuine members of this fellowship by being *imitators of the God* to whom we are now
2 related *as children beloved* of the Father for our likness to him;
and you must *dispose yourselves in practical life by* the motive
and behavior of *love,* taking *the Christ* of God as source and
example in all our relations *just as* he *loved you* before you
loved or knew him *and* expressed that love in that he *gave him-*
self in sacrificial mediatorial devotion *in behalf of us.* For we
must all think of the meaning for ourselves when we think of

how our Christ became *an offering and sacrifice to God,* taking
upon himself in living devotion even unto death the place of
all the sacrifices and offerings of the ceremonial systems, and
was in this entirely satisfactory to God *as a sweet smelling odor*
coming up to God from humanity through the atoning Christ,
to speak in the analogy of the sacrifices by which Israel was
made acceptable to God.
3 It is most important to free yourselves wholly from social
sins and keep clean in body and mind. *Fornication and every
form of impurity or sexual excess, let it not* so much as *be mentioned in your* Christian *groups, just as is* the *appropriate* course
4 *for people consecrated to God in Christ.* The same rule must
hold *also* in the case of talking about *shameful conduct, and* of
senseless talk, or of *language easily turned* to base suggestion—
these are all forms of speech *which are unbecoming;* but rather
by contrast our speech should be *readily a-means-of-grace.
For keep this constantly in your practical knowledge; every
fornicator, or impure person, or man-of insatiable*-passion,
who is, in fact, nothing less than *a sex-idolator, is barred from
having any share in that Kingdom* which is founded and constituted by the Christ *and* which under the dominion *of the
Christ,* is also the realm *of God.*
6 *Let nobody lead you astray with words empty* of truth and
reason with reference to all this category of impurity and sex
expression, *for it is because of* just *these things* that *the* very
wrath of God comes upon the sons of disobedience, men who
in selfish and fleshly abandon are so ready to disobey all moral
and religious restraints as rightly to be called children of dis-
7 obedience. *Do not, then, permit yourselves to become partners
in their* shame *and sharers* in their doom.
8 It is necessary to take a very positive attitude with reference to all this, *for* you know all too well that *there was a time,*
now to be emphatically kept in the past, when *you were* so
gripped in the ways of moral darkness as to be yourselves part
of that *darkness, whereas now in the Lord* ye are *light,* being
so identified with him as to share his nature as the Light of
men; and being such you are to *conduct your lives as children
of Light.* And such conduct cannot include these old sins
9 of the flesh, *because the fruit of* (*produced by*) *the Light* con-
10 sists *in all* forms of *goodness, righteousness, and truth,* to produce which you must *be constantly testing what is well-
11 pleasing to the Lord* by reference to the nature of Light in God.
And do not make common cause with the works that are
products *of the darkness, those* works *that are without fruit;*

but rather, by the *contrast* of your own fruitful living, *even*
12 *expose* their revolting nature. It needs exposing, *for the things*
which are carried on by them in secret it is shameful even to
13 *speak of, but all things when exposed by the light are revealed*
for what they really are, *for the revealing light is everything*
14 in disclosing the true nature of conduct and the true character
of men. It is *in accord with this* that *we have the saying:*

> *"Arise, thou sleeping one,*
> *And stand up from among the dead;*
> *And the Christ will shine upon thee."*

15 With so much involved, *therefore,* in your manner of life,
watch sharply how you conduct yourselves, living *not as men*
16 *lacking wisdom but as wise men, buying up the opportunity* for
right and helpful living when it appears in the market of life,
for the days are evil, so that occasions for creative activity are
17 limited and require eager seeking. *Because of this* situation,
do not allow yourselves to *become lacking in wisdom, but study*
out what is the will of your Lord in all circumstances so that
18 you may know how to conduct yourselves. *And do not get-*
muddled-up with wine, a course *wherein* the exhilaration
produces not increased power but *reckless unreliability.* By
contrast, in order to be lifted out of the dull normality of drab
living, *allow yourselves to be filled,* not physically but in your
19 *spiritual being,* which the Holy Spirit is ready to do; and give
expression to your exaltation *by speaking within yourselves*
in psalms, hymns, and Spirit-inspired songs, singing and mak-
20 *ing instrumental-music with* all *your heart to your Lord, at all*
times and over all things giving thanks, in the name of our
Lord Jesus Christ, to his, and through him *our God and Father.*
21 In carrying forward this Christian way of life, with understanding according to the will of our Lord and as his one Body,
and remembering that we are members of one another in interdependence, we must be faithfully *subjecting ourselves to one*
another in reverent awe of Christ in whom and for whom we
now live.
22 *All wives* will order their lives in fitting subjection *to their*
own husbands as required in this relation in duty *to the Lord,*
23 for subjection to our Lord includes loyal living in the home.
This subjecting herself by the wife is proper, *because a hus-*
band is head of his wife in the mutual arrangement of the
family, *even in the spirit and manner that the Christ is head*
24 *of his Church, he* who is *Savior of his Body. But,* while the
Christ is savior of the Church, and the husband should have

this savior responsibility for his wife, *just as the Church properly* and necessarily *subjects herself to the Christ* for her salvation, and realizing the full meaning of the relation of the Christ and his Church, *in the same way also,* in the relation and purpose of husband and wife, must *wives subject themselves to their husbands in everything.*

25 Now, *you husbands,* put in such relation to your wives in
the economy of the family, after the method of the Savior
for growing his Social Body, *love your wives even as Christ*
bestowed his love on his Church and gave himself up in life
26 and death *in behalf of her:* (1) *in order that he might cleanse*
her with the bath of water, symbolically applied in baptism
which in our analogy represents the nuptial bath of the bride
27 in marriage, *and set her apart in purity;* (2) *in order that he*
might himself, as loving, redeeming, and devoted Lord, *set his*
Church in full glory at his side all his very own, not having a
speck or wrinkle or any of such blemishing things that would
detract from perfection; *but* (3) *in order that she might be holy*
and subject to no sort of *criticism.*

28 *In the same way* as the Christ assumes the responsibility for
his Church-bride and spares himself nothing that will realize
his ideal, and so devotes himself to his Church-bride, *are hus-*
bands under obligation to love their individual wives, account
ing them and treating them *as their own personal bodies,* as
the Church is the Body of the Christ. *The man* in *loving his*
own precious wife is loving himself, for he is completed and per-
29 fected only in her. Hence the call to perfect love of one's own
wife, *for no one ever hated his own flesh, but rather* does every-
one *nourish* and *cherish it;* and this includes loving and cherishing his wife. We set up the standard for the husband as that of
30 caring for his wife *just as also the Christ* nourishes and
cherishes *his Church, because we are members of his Body,*
and consequently should understand and adopt his principles
in our relations to one another within his Church.

31 *In the face of this* ideal, this essential principle and its embodiment in Christ and his Church, the original and abiding
standard, announced by God from the beginning is, that *a man*
shall leave father and mother and deliberately *become insepa-*
rably attached to his wife, the one to the other, *and the two*
of them *shall come-to-be one unit-of-flesh. This divinely*
32 *declared ideal is exalted,* to be sure, *but, so far as I am con-*
cerned, I insist on it as the true Christian ideal: for the husband, *up to* the standard of *Christ; and* for the wife, *up to*

the standard of *the Church;* thus for the two united, up to the perfect union sought for Christ and Church.

33 *To reiterate in summary, then, let all of you, one by one,* individually, *love each thus his own wife as himself and,* as for *the wife,* this standard provides *that she reverence her husband,* as she can do when he is such a husband as is enjoined in Christ.

CHAPTER VI

1 Now *to the children: Give obedient heed as subject to your*
parents in the Lord, who is the all encompassing and constraining power and purpose in all Christian relationships, *for*
this is the right course for children. *"Honor thy father and*
2 *thy mother," the very first commandment* for children, which
3 God in giving his law to his people *set in a promise: "in order*
that it may turn out well for thee, and thou mayest have long
life tenure upon the earth."

4 *You fathers also,* on your part, *do not anger your children by provoking* them, *but rather give them progressive nourishment in* the *discipline and instruction proper* for parents who accept themselves and their children as *in the Lord,* and relate themselves to their children as all existing in and as constrained by the Lord, accepting the claims of his love and redemptive purpose.

5 *You who are bond-slaves, give obedient heed as subject*
to those who in human relations are your lords, serving
with reverence and the caution of fear, in genuine readiness
of your heart, always thinking of yourselves in this, as in all
conduct in all relations, *as* giving your service *to your Christ;*
and thus *not* behaving *on the basis of service under the*
watchful *eye* of an exacting master, *as those who must please*
men or suffer penalty; but rather meet the demands of your
station *as bond-slaves of Christ,* your true and ultimate
7 Master, for whose sake you are *doing what God wills, from*
the soul, serving with generous disposition; as doing it really
8 *for your Lord and not* primarily *for men; keeping* always
the consciousness that each man, regardless of his status in
the social order, *will get back in compensation from the Lord*
whatever good thing he may do, whether as he serves the
Lord he is in the social order *a slave* or *a free man.*

9 Now *you who are masters also* must accept the Christian principles: *Do in relation to them*—your slaves—*the same things,* in the same spirit, having the same attitude, *keeping* always *the consciousness that both their and your* one

common *Master is in heaven,* whence all of us are always seen and judged by the perfect standards of heaven, *and* keeping in mind *that partiality on account of superficial appearances has no place with him.*

10 *Of the rest* which the heart would like to stress concerning the worthy response in living to the high calling of God in Christ Jesus, this in summary conclusion: *Be continuously empowered* by maintaining your strength and meeting all your situations *in* your united oneness with our *Lord and in the might* which comes to us out *of his strength.*
11 *Put on the complete armor,* every piece of it, *which God provides* for us, *with the purpose of your being able to stand your ground in the face of the devices of the devil.*

12 All this divine provision is necessary, and our making fullest and most careful use of it all is essential *because for us the conflict is not merely against blood and flesh,* no mere human warfare, *but against the* real or imagined *realms, against the* real or putative spheres of *authorities,* against *the world-rulers* by which speculative philosophies bring men under the dominion *of this* present era of intellectual and moral *darkness, against the spiritual* influences *of evil* which operate *in the heavenly* relations of our souls and our society. Thus our struggle is against all that order of thought and reality which wars against the souls of men and corrupts our relations to God's righteousness, against our own spiritual realization, and against the reign of God
13 in human life and history.

On account of this all-important spiritual warfare which faces us in accepting and fulfilling God's calling to us in the redeeming Christ, and because of the powerful and subtle nature of the opposition we must overcome, *take up* in detail *the complete armor* provided in the saving plan *of our God in order that you may be powerful for holding your ground in the day that is evil* in bitterest struggle, whether now or whenever it shall come upon you, *and* may be able *after having carried every phase* of the bitter but glorious fight *through* to complete victory *to stand* in command of the field.

14 *Take-your-stand, therefore,* on the field of conflict *belted around your thighs with the girdle of true integrity; and clothed with the breastplate of righteousness* of character
15 and conduct; *having your feet shod,* for firm footing and protection against injury, *with that preparation* for Christian struggle which is brought to us in *the gospel of peace* with
16 God and godly peace with men; *and having taken up along*

with all the rest *the shield of the* full *faith* in God's assurance
and his effective presence in you, *in which you will have*
the power, by catching them in that shield, *to extinguish all*
the darts shot at you *by the Evil One, the* darts which in his
malignant efforts to destroy you *have been* treated with tar
17 and pitch and *set on fire* as they were shot at you. *And take*
from God the conscious assurance of the *salvation process*
for your *head protection helmet,* and *the sword provided by*
the Holy *Spirit, which is the word of God* with which you
are to do all your aggressive fighting. Carry on the conflict
in continuous prayer by means of every form of prayer and
petition offered *in every situation* and always in co-operation
with the Spirit, who prays with us and for us, *and ever being*
on the watch for (it) the occasion calling for prayer, *with*
continuous application of energy and petition with reference
to all the consecrated people of Christ.
19 *And* be certain to keep praying *in behalf of me,* asking
that to me there may be given *freedom of utterance in the*
opening of my mouth by the Holy Spirit so as *to make known*
20 with clear fulness *that divine inner meaning of the gospel, in*
behalf of which I am under necessity of *carrying on my work*
as Christ's *ambassador in a chain,* since I am enduring these
years of imprisonment just because I stand for the universality of the gospel on equal terms to all races and conditions
of men. Yes, pray for me, *that in (it)* carrying on my work
I may have bold freedom as it is necessary for me to speak.
21 *In order that you may know clearly, even you, my affairs,*
what I am doing, Tychicus will inform you as to all things,
the beloved brother and faithful minister to me *in* the *bonds*
which unite us as both serving *the Lord, whom I have sent*
22 *to you for just this* purpose, *that you may know the* conditions and facts *about us and in order that he may encourage*
your hearts, which might be troubled by uncertainty and
ignorance concerning what has befallen me in this long
period when you could not know how it was faring with me
and my mission.
23 I send my benediction, *peace to* you who are *my brethren*
in the Lord and his work, *and love* to dominate all your contacts and experiences, *along with faith*—may they come to you
24 *from Father God* and *Lord Jesus Christ. May the grace of*
God be *with all who love our Lord Jesus Christ in* a love
that is *incapable* of *being corrupted.*

Author's Translation

No task can be more impossible than faithful translation. Correspondence between vocabularies of two languages is limited. Thought content and variations of connotation differ widely between words that correspond in a general way. Idioms are often impossible to tranfer from one language to another. "Word pictures" can be reproduced in part only. The task is to ascertain just what the original writer sought to express and then to find the nearest possible form in which to convey his meaning into the new language. Variations in syntax constitute another difficulty. As between the Greek and the English, punctuation poses a problem. The extensive inflection in Greek and its remarkable wealth of connectives and particles make it possible to use sentence structure with entire clarity where the relative poverty of English in these elements demands resort to other methods.

Paul, with a mind very cogent in its thinking and with capacity for holding in balanced relation the parts and connections of complicated ideas, was led to use of long sentences. In Ephesians, half of chapter 1 is put in a single sentence; and there are others almost as long and as full of ideas. Literal translation being only partially and inadequately possible, should it be attempted? Many translations of the New Testament do not undertake it. They differ widely in the fidelity with which they reproduce the forms of thought and the freedom with which they transfer the ideas in quite other English forms. Some (as Weymouth) strive for fullest fidelity to the Greek consistent with clarity of English. Others (as the Twentieth Century) are often little better than paraphrase.

Here as closely literal a translation is offered as the author finds possible while making clear what he understands to be the thought, and the thought-forms, the spirit and the expression of the apostle. His greatest difficulty and hesitation were in seeking to preserve in English the sentence structure of the most approved manuscripts. This has sometimes not been possible without resort to devices for making the meaning clear. The author is aware that consequently the English is sometimes awkward, not to say rough. In the much fuller expository paraphrase, which precedes the translation, the thought context has been supplied, the sentences of the original have been broken up freely, and the reading, it is hoped, flows somewhat smoothly.

Reasons for undertaking so nearly literal a rendering are chiefly to enable the English reader to see and feel, so far as possible, the underlying Greek and even more the heart and mind of the great apostle. By comparing the translation here with that of the King James Version, the discerning reader will be able better to sense the Greek idiom and syntax and, it is hoped, to catch the vibrating enthusiasm of Paul.

In order to make clearer the longer sentences, the grammatical connections and the sometimes unfamiliar vocabulary that reproduces the Greek, several devices have been adopted. Painstaking care in punctuation, especially in the long sentences, is relied upon. Of course the older Greek manuscripts have next to no punctuation. Where several words in English must be employed to render a single word compounded of two or more Greek words, this is often indicated by hyphens connecting the English words. Where, as often, the tense or the voice of a Greek verb is important for the meaning, more than one word is required in the English.

In Greek certain forms, particles, and position in a sentence indicate emphasis which must be indicated in different ways in translation. No resort has been had to Italics or black face type. What may seem excessive use of conjunctions and other connectives is due to the Greek sense of continuity, relation, and progress of thought, which are far less evident in usual English composition.

Sometimes the condensed Greek expression, clear in the original by reason of grammatical agreement, etc., requires supplying words in English. In this translation supplied words are in parentheses.

AUTHOR'S TRANSLATION

CHAPTER I

Paul, representative of Christ Jesus, sent forth through an action of the will of God, to those who are dedicated, who are (in Ephesus) and are faithful in Christ Jesus: (2) grace to you and peace from God our Father and from Lord Jesus (the) Christ.

(3) Blessed be God (who is) also Father of our Lord Jesus Christ, the One who blessed us in every blessing (that is) spiritual, in our heavenly relationships, in Christ; (4) even as he chose us in him before (his) projecting the world-order, for us to be dedicated and blameless in his full view: in (his) love having already marked us off for sonship-adoption unto him, through Jesus Christ, on the ground of the good-pleasure of his act-of-will; (6) for the end of the glorifying praise of his grace in that he made us objects of his grace in his Beloved; (7) in whom we have the-redemption-experience through his blood, (even) the bearing away of our transgressions; (all this) on the scale of the richness of his grace (8) which he caused to flow-in upon us in every-form of wisdom and discernment, (9) thereby causing us to know the inner intent of his will, (which was) based on his good-pleasure, which he projected in him (Christ the Beloved); (10) with the intention of (establishing) a stewardship of administration for the full realization of (the meaning of) the ages-of-history, for bringing all things under one headship in the Christ, the things upon the heavens and the things upon the earth: (11) in him in whom we were made a heritage, having been previously marked off (as such) in accordance with (the) plan of the one who produces all things by his energy, working according to the counsel of his own will; (12) with the objective of our being the means of the praise of his glory, we who had all along been cherishing hope in the Christ; (13) in whom you, too, upon hearing the true divine message (as embodied in) the good news that salvation is for you, and upon having put your trust in him, received upon you the promised Spirit, as God's seal, the Holy Spirit; (14) who is (thereby) a pledge of our being (God's) heritage, destined for full redemption of that with which he continues his work; unto the praise of his glory.

(15) On account of all this, I on-my-part, having heard about the faith in the Lord Jesus that obtains among you, and your love which extends to all the saints.

(16) do not cease in my rejoicing over you; making definite mention (of you) in my praying; (17) that the God of our Lord Jesus Christ, the Father of glory, may give to you a spirit of insight and revelation evidenced in exact-knowledge of him; (18) your heart's eyes fully-enlightened so that you may know-by-insight what is his (God's) hope (in the people and plan) of his calling; what the wealth of the (his) glory of (in) his heritage in his saints; (19) and what the more-than-sufficient greatness of his dynamic power (which he brings) into (operation in) us who continuously-trust him, (which power is) on the scale of the energy of the active-grip of his strength (20) which he put-forth-energetically in the Christ when he raised him out-from-among dead-bodies, and set him on his right hand in the heavenly-realms, (21) clear above every (form and order of) rule and authority and power and lordship, and every name that is named, not only in this present age but also in the age that is about-to-come; (22) and all things he put-in ordered-arrangement under his feet, and (the Christ) himself he gave to the Church as its supreme, exclusive Head, (23) because it is his Body, the full expression of the one who is bringing to full realization all things in all respects.

CHAPTER II

(1) And you, too, (God raised up) when you were dead by reason of your failures and your sins, (2) in which it was formerly your habit-to-conduct-your-lives, in correspondence with the age of this world; in accord with the one who administers the authority of the atmosphere, the spirit which is even now exerting-himself-effectively in those who are sons of disobedience, (3) among whom we all, too, once lived-our-lives in the impulsive desires of our unregenerate-human-nature and of our own private notions, and (thus) we were by nature children of wrath even as are the others:—(4) but God, because of his being rich in mercy, on account of his great love with which he loved us (5) even while we were, by reason of our transgressions, (spiritually) dead bodies, made us alive-along-with the Christ—by grace you have been brought-into-the-saved-state—(6) and he raised us up-along with him, and along-with-him (as included in Christ Jesus) he set-us-down in the heavenly-realms; (7) in order that in the oncoming ages he might-have-a-demonstration of the transcendent riches of his gracious-nature, in the fact of his bestowing-grace upon us in Christ Jesus. (8) For it is by grace that you have-been-brought-into-salvation, by faith; and this experience (did) not (originate) from you, (it is) the gift of God; (9) not by-way-of

works, so that no individual may boast. (10) For we (as saved) are a product of his, having been created in Christ Jesus for good works, which God made-ready-beforehand as the sphere in which we should-conduct-our-lives.

(11) Do you, therefore, keep-constantly-in-mind that at one time you, the Gentiles in flesh distinction, those called "uncircumcised" by that which calls itself "circumcision," (a) hand-made (distinction, existing merely) in (the) flesh—, (12) that you were at that time without a Christ, in alienated-exclusion from the spiritual-commonwealth of Israel and outsiders from the standpoint of the convenants of the promise, not cherishing any hope and without-God in the world-order. (13) But now, by strong contrast, in Christ Jesus you who were then "at a distance," have come to be "near" in the blood of the Christ. (14) For he is himself our "peace," the one who made the two (separate groups) one, and by breaking down the separating wall of enmity which-made-fragments (of an ideal unity), in his flesh (15) made ineffective the law of formal-commands expressed in dogmas, in order that in his person he might create (out of the material of) the two (race groups) into one new human race, thus producing peace, (16) and (thus) might harmonize the two divisions, as one body, to God, by means of his cross; by it definitely putting-to-death the (racial) enmity. (17) And having come (with this purpose, power and persuasion) "he proclaimed as good news peace to" you, "those far off, and peace to those near" (Isa. 57:19); (18) because through him we have our way-of-approach, both (groups of us), in one Spirit unto the Father (of the Christ and of ourselves in him).

(19) Well, then, you are by consequence no longer interlopers, mere-sojourners (in the Christian calling), but truly are fellow-citizens in the body of the saints and members of our God's family-group; (20) having been erected directly upon the foundation of the apostles and prophets, (21) Christ Jesus himself being the chief corner-stone, in relation to whom each several building, being harmoniously wrought in with the rest contributes its increment of growth toward a temple holy in the Lord; (22) in which you, on your part, are-in-the-process-of-harmonious-construction into a dwelling place of God in the Spirit.

CHAPTER III

(1) For the sake of this (work of God) I, Paul the prisoner of the Christ, Jesus, in the interest of you, the Gentile peoples—(2) if, indeed, as surely, you heard-so-as-to-understand the stewardship of God's grace which was given to me with reference to you, (3)

that by the method of a revelation the inner-purpose (of God in the Christ) was made known to me, even as I have briefly expressed it already; (4) by facing which (statement) you will be able, if you read-it-carefully, to perceive my comprehending-understanding in the divine-meaning of the Christ, (5) (a mystery) which for other generations was not made known to the sons of men as now it was disclosed to his holy apostles and prophets in the Spirit: (namely) (6) that the Gentile peoples are a joint-heritage (of God); and along-with (the Jews) a corporate body; and common-sharers (with the Jews) of the promise in Christ Jesus, by means of the gospel; (7) of which (gospel) I got to be a minister on the ground and in the measure of God's self-initiated gift of grace, which was imparted to me by means of and in the measure of the active working of his power. (8) Even to me, the less-than-least of all saints, there was given this undeserved (double) honor and capacity: to bring to the heathen peoples as good news the wealth of the Christ, that is beyond all defining; (9) also, to bring-to-light what is the method-of-stewardship for the divine-secret which has been hidden-away from (the beginning of) the ages in the God who created all that is; (10) (God's provision) in order that now through the Church the many-sided wisdom of God may be made known to the ordered systems of rule and authority in the heavenly-realms; (11) (all) according to a plan of the ages which he projected in the Christ, Jesus, our Lord; (12) in whom we have our boldness (in preaching) and successful approach (to men) in assured confidence through our faith in him. (13) Wherefore I beg that there will be no unhappy despondency in (the fact of) my afflictions in behalf of you, inasmuch as this is your glory.

(14) For this cause (see verse 1) I bow my knees before the Father, (15) from whom every family-group in heaven and upon earth derives its name, (16) that he will grant to you, in correspondence with his wealth in glory, to be made so mightily strong by his Spirit (coming) into (and working in) your inner man (17) that the Christ may have-residence in your hearts through your faith, you being throughly-rooted and firmly-grounded in love, (18) to the further end that you may-be-fully-competent to grasp in connection with all the saints, what is the breadth, and length, and height, and depth, (19) even to know the knowledge-transcending love expressed in the Christ; with the ultimate end that you may (as a corporate body) be filled up to all the fulness of God.

(20) Now to him who is powerful beyond all things to do overwhelmingly more than we are asking or conceiving-in-our-minds, on the basis of his power which is-continuously-working within us,

(21) to him be the glory in the Church and in Christ Jesus unto all the generations of the age of the ages. Amen..

CHAPTER IV

I, therefore, call-you-along, I the prisoner in the Lord, to order-your-life worthily of the calling with which you were called, (2) with unfailing humility and meekness, with unflagging spiritual endurance, mutually-continuing-the-support of one another in love, (3) constantly eager to guard, by maintaining, the unity of the Spirit (which he aims at and produces) in the unifying-bond of peace: (4) One Body and One Spirit, exactly corresponding to (the further fact) that you were called in (God's) One Hope of your calling, (5) One Lord, One Faith, One Baptism; (6) One God, even Father of all, who is over all and through all, and in all.

(7) And to each one of us was his grace given in accordance with the measure of the voluntary-giving of the Christ. (8) Hence the saying (Psalm 68:18):

"Going up on high he led captive a band of captives,
He gave gifts to mankind."

(9) Now the expression, "he went up," what does it imply except that he also came down into the lower realms, of the earth? (10) The one who came down is himself also the one who went up on-beyond all the heavens, with the purpose of bringing all things to completeness.

(11) And he thus gave some men for the function of missionary-apostles; some to function as prophets; some with the function of evangelizing (from the missionary centers); and some who should be pastors and teachers; (12) with a view to the corporate-cordinating of the saints for active service; (looking) unto the building-up of the Body of the Christ (13) until we, all-of-us-together, reach that oneness which is (truly characteristic) of the faith and of our full-knowledge of the Son of God, unto mature manhood, even unto the measure of the stature of the full-self-realization of the Christ; (14) which involves that we be no longer babes, (or like) waves surging aimlessly and tossed about by every wind of teaching, determined by the mere gamble of mere men, (thus being) subject to the craftiness that looks toward deceitful error: (15) but, instead, being faithfully-true in the realm of love, we are to be constantly effecting growth, in all respects, into him who is the Head, Christ, (16) from whom as source all the Body, progressively being wrought into harmonious unity and firmly knit together by means of every contact for the supply (of his grace), according to the active functioning in due measure of each several part, (this Body) effects the continuous growth of the Body as it builds itself up in

(the processes of) love.

(17) Here, then, is my affirmation and testimony in the Lord: that you are to conduct-your-lives no longer after the manner in which the heathen do actually conduct-their-lives in the insane folly of their mind, (18) being darkened in their mental operations, having alienated themselves from the life which God supplies, this by reason of the ignorance which is characteristic of them on account of the hardening of their hearts; (19) who, having lost the sense of moral shame, abandoned themselves to entire indecency for the active practice of every form of uncleanness with insatiable-desire.

(20) But it was not thus that you learned the Christ, (21) assuming that it was actually he whom you heard and that you were instructed in him in full accord with truth as incorporated in Jesus: (22) that you are to strip yourselves of the old unregenerate humanity, characterizing your former way-of-conducting-yourselves, that old human nature that is ever in process of corruption, according to its natural tendencies to deceit; (23) further, that you are to enter upon a continuous experience of renewal of the spirit of your mind; (24) and also that you are to clothe yourselves with the new human nature which, corresponding to (the character of) God, was created in the righteousness and holiness characteristic of the truth.

(25) Wherefore, definitely-putting-away what is false do you all individually speak truth as each deals with his neighbor, because we are mutually members each of the other's selfhood. (26) Get angry and still do not sin; do not permit even one sun to go down on your passing-anger, (27) nor give standing room to the devil. (28) The man who has a habit of stealing, let him no longer steal; but rather let him become-a-toiler, working with his own hands in some good line so that he may have something to share with the one who has actual need. (29) Every word (that may suggest itself to you but is) corrupt, let it not escape out of your mouth; on the contrary, if any (word is available) good for the constructive use where there is need (speak it), in order that it may contribute grace to those who hear. (30) And do not grieve the Spirit, the Holy (Spirit), God's (Spirit), in whom you were definitely sealed as destined for the day of complete redemption.

(31) Every form of irritability, and quick-temper, and wrath, and railing, and reviling, let it be put away from you, along with every kind of maliciousness. (32) And make yourselves graciously useful in your relations to one another, being of good disposition, being gracious to one another even just as your God was gracious to you in Christ.

Chapter V

(1) Become, therefore, definitely imitators of our God as children beloved; (2) and so conduct-your-lives in love, even as the Christ loved you and gave himself over in behalf of us, an offering and a sacrifice to God acceptible as a satisfying odor.

(3) Furthermore, fornication and every form of impurity or sexual excess, let no one of them even be mentioned among you, just as is appropriate for saints; (4) as also applies in the case of shameful conduct and senseless talk or language easily turned to evil suggestion, which things are unbecoming; rather by contrast (our appropriate speech is) readily-a-means-of-grace. (5) For know this by constant observation, that every fornicator, or impure person, or man of insatiable passion, who is a sex-idolater, is barred from having any share in the Kingdom of the Christ and God. (6) Let nobody lead you astray (about this) with empty words, for it is through these practices that God's wrath is continuously coming upon the sons of disobedience. (7) Do not, therefore, permit yourselves to become sharers of their (shame and doom): (8) for you were formerly darkness, but now are light in the Lord: you must conduct-your-lives as children of Light (9) — for the product of Light consists in every form of goodness, and righteousness, and truth —, (10) continuously making test (so as to know) what is well-pleasing to the Lord; (11) and never participate in those fruitless works of Darkness, but rather even be ever exposing them, (12) for the things that are carried on by them in secret it is shameful even to mention: (13) but all sorts of things, when exposed by the Light become evident (for what they are), for the revealing Light is everything. (14) Hence the saying:

"Arise, thou sleeping one,
And stand up from among the dead,
And upon thee shall the Christ shine."

(15) Keep a sharp look-out, therefore, how you conduct-yourselves, not as men lacking wisdom, but as wise men, (16) buying up the opportunity, because the days are evil. (17) On account of this situation do not allow yourselves to become lacking in wisdom, but study-out what is the will of your Lord. (18) And do not get-muddled-up with wine in which is reckless unreliability, but allow yourselves to be filled in your spiritual being, (19) speaking to yourselves in psalms, hymns and Spirit-

inspired songs, singing and making instrumental music heartily to the Lord, (20) at all times and over all things giving thanks in the name of our Lord Jesus Christ to his and our Father-God, (the while) (21) subjecting yourselves to one another in reverent-consideration of Christ.

(22) All wives (are to subject themselves) to their own husbands as to the Lord, (23) for a husband is head of his wife even as the Christ (is) head of his Church, in his case Savior of his Body. (24) Still, as the Church holds herself subject to the Christ, in the same sense also should the wives (hold themselves subject) to their husbands in everything.

(25) You husbands: love your wives steadily, just as the Christ also fixed-his-love on his Church, and gave himself up in her behalf, (26) in order that her (only) he might set-apart in purity, having purified her in the (nuptial) water bath, in analogy: (27) in order that he might himself place his Church alongside himself his very own, all glorious, not having a speck, or a wrinkle, or any of such blemishing things; but in order that she might be holy and subject to no criticism. (28) In the same way husbands are under obligation steadily-to-love their own wives, as their own individual bodies. The man in loving his own precious wife is loving himself; (29) for no one ever hated his own flesh, but, on the contrary, (every one) nourishes and cherishes it, even as the Christ his Church, (30) for we are members of his Body. (31) In view of this standard a man shall leave father and mother and be-inseparably-united unto his wife, and they shall become, the two, one unit-of-flesh.

(32) This ideal is exalted, but I insist, up to Christ and up to the Church; (33) and, furthermore: do you all individually, each one keep-on-loving his own wife as himself, and the wife may she respect her husband.

CHAPTER VI

(1) The children: give-obedient-hearing to your parents in the Lord, for this is the right course. (2) "Honor thy father and mother," which, note, is as a commandment the first, set in a promise: (3) "in order that it may prove well with thee and that thou mayest have-long-life-tenure upon the earth." (4) And you fathers: do not irritate your children by provoking (them), but instead give them progressive nourishment with discipline and instruction proper in the Lord.

(5) You (who are) slaves: give-obedient-heed as subject to those who in human relations are your lords, with reverence and

the caution of fear, in genuine readiness of your heart, as to your Christ; (6) not on the basis of service under watchful eyes, as having to please men, but rather as slaves of Christ doing what God desires, from the very soul, (7) serving with generous disposition as for your Lord, and not (primarily) for men; (8) keeping the consciousness that each man will get-back-in-compensation from the Lord whatever good thing he may do whether as slave or as freeman. (9) And you masters: do the same in relation to them (the slaves), avoiding domineering threatening, keeping-the-consciousness that both their and your common Master is in heaven, and that partiality based on appearances has no place with him.

(10) Of what remains (to be said, only this): receive-continuous-empowering in the Lord, and in the active-power which comes from his strength. (11) Put on the complete armor which our God provides with a view to your being able to maintain-your-position against the devices of the devil: (12) because for us the conflict is not (merely) against blood and flesh, but against the powers, against the authorities, against the imperial rulers of the present-age darkness, against the spiritual aspects of wickedness in the heavenly-relations. (13) On account of this, take up the complete armor which our God provides, in order that you may be powerful for holding-your-ground in the evil day, and after having carried every phase of the conflict to complete victory, to stand firm.

(14) Take your position, then, belted around your thighs with the girdle of integrity, and having put on the breastplate of righteous-character, (15) and having shod your feet with the preparation which the gospel of peace affords, (16) and along with all these having taken up the shield which firm faith affords, with which you will have the ability to extinguish all the arrows of the evil one which have been set ablaze with burning pitch: (17) and the helmet of assured salvation you must get, and the sword which the Spirit provides and uses, which is God's word; (18) (stand and win thus) by means of every use of prayer and petition, continuously praying on every occasion in the Spirit, and ever-on-the-watch for it (the occasion calling for prayer) with steady devotion-of energy; including petition concerning all the saints; (19) and certainly in behalf of me: that to me a proper message may be given, that with the opening of my mouth I may openly make known the essential-meaning of the gospel, (20) in the interest of which I am serving-as-(Christ's)

ambassador in a chain; (pray) that in it (all) I may have bold freedom as it becomes necessary for me to talk.

(21) In order that you may know clearly, you especially, my affairs, what I am doing, all this Tychicus will make known to you, our beloved brother and faithful helper in the Lord, (22) whom I send unto you for this very purpose, that he may make known to you the things concerning us and (thus) may encourage your hearts.

(23) Peace to the brethren and love with abundant faith, from God (the) Father and (from the) Lord Jesus Christ. (24) His grace with all who are maintaining love for our Lord Jesus Christ in incorruptness.